A Question of Evidence

*Books by Christopher Berry-Dee
and Robin Odell*

DAD, HELP ME PLEASE
A QUESTION OF EVIDENCE

Christopher Berry-Dee
with Robin Odell

A QUESTION
OF EVIDENCE

Who killed the Babes in the Wood?

W H ALLEN

First published in Great Britain in 1991 by
W. H. Allen
an imprint of Virgin Publishing
338 Ladbroke Grove
London W10 5AH

Cataloguing in Publication data available from the British Library

ISBN 1–85227–292–9

Typeset in 11/14 Meridien
by Phoenix Photosetting, Chatham, Kent
Printed and bound in Great Britain by
Mackays of Chatham PLC, Chatham, Kent

Dedicated to

Karen Hadaway and Nicola Fellows

Contents

Acknowledgements

I owe much to the many who have listened to my endless enquiries and who have with courtesy tried to help. I wish to express my gratitude to Michelle and Lee Hadaway; Susan and Barrie Fellows; Russell Bishop and his mother, Sylvia; Ian and Kevin Heffron; Mick Dawes and Councillor Gordon Wingate, for their unfailing support.

For information and advice on the medical, legal and police aspects of the Babes in the Wood case I am indebted to Lord Lane, Lord Chief Justice of England; Professor Derrick Pounder; Dr Denis Power; D. Neylan and Dr Anthony Peabody (Aldermaston); former Detective Sergeant Bill Swan; Dr Anthony Harbott; the Law Society; the Lord Chancellor's Department and the Sussex Constabulary; the Home Office Prison Department; the Metropolitan Police; Lewes Crown Court; and Hibbert & Saunders, court shorthand writers.

For local background and social details I am grateful to Jim and Rosalind Stevenson; the residents of Moulsecoomb and the people of Brighton; R. W. French; the Brighton & Hove Bus and Coach Company; the *Evening Argus*; Jeremy Britton (TVS); the *Brighton & Hove Leader*; Andrew Bowden MBE, MP; Brighton Borough Council and Library; author and Brighton historian Clifford Musgrave; and Initial Contract Services Limited.

Very special thanks must go to the Rt Hon Margaret

Thatcher MP and the Prime Minister's Office; the *Southern Evening Echo*; Southern Sound; BBC Radio Solent; and Ocean Sound.

The book would have taken so much longer to research had it not been for my wife Tracey, who spent hours studying the case files and always gave unfailing support; David Cox, who provided a warm car and safe driving for research trips; my close friends Bill and Julie Patterson, who lifted my spirits when they were low; Patrick and May Dee; David and Sonia Davey; Susanne McDadd; Gill Gibbins; my agents Peter Robinson and Mike Shaw of Curtis Brown, London; Sarah Roberts for the typing; and W. H. Allen/Virgin, my committed publishers.

Last, but by no means least, I would like to express my gratitude to my colleague Robin Odell, who never lost faith in this book and who always, selflessly, supported the researching and writing of it. His contribution was invaluable and he gave me much guidance at every stage.

Christopher Berry-Dee
Curdridge,
February 1991.

Illustrations

Prologue

In 1989, W. H. Allen commissioned me to write a book called *Unsolved Murders*. The brief was to cover at least 50 killings where the files were still open and bring them once again to the public eye. The Wild Park murders, in 1986, of Karen Hadaway and Nicola Fellows, both aged nine, were to be part of that collection and as a matter of course I approached a local Brighton newspaper, the *Evening Argus*. Jim Hatley, a former staff reporter, made available the *Argus*'s entire file of newscuttings for my initial research; he walked with me to the scene of the crime and to the locations involved throughout this book. Finally, he asked me if I would like to visit the graves.

Bear Road Cemetery is one of several that lie to the north-east of Brighton. Driving east along the congested Lewes Road past Brighton race course and on towards the not-too-distant suburb of Woodingdean, we branched off right down Bear Road and left the hubbub behind. Karen and Nicola lie in a double grave set into a grassy knoll overlooking the sprawling town. On a clear day one can just see the English Channel, with Brighton's piers and Grand Parade framed between the bleak mass of a general hospital and the rolling green fairways of a golf course. But on that first visit the weather had closed in around the hill with a grey mantle of low cloud and drizzle. A slight wind was rising in the swaying yews, heralding the approach of a storm. It was cold and damp.

Jim and I stood for a moment in respect, then I drew nearer and noticed that someone had propped a card against the headstone: 'Happy Birthday, darling. You are with your mum and dad every minute of the day.' It had been Karen's twelfth birthday a few days before.

A school photograph of each child was set into the marble headstone. Flowers covered the green and blue chippings; a few of the girls' toys had been lovingly placed for comfort. They were rain-soaked and in disarray. I knelt down and set them nearer the girls, then stood back and quietly took in the feelings of sadness that nearly overwhelmed me.

That evening I sat, morose, deep in thought. Rain beat on the roof of my cottage. I glanced through the window to the garden, but I saw Bear Road Cemetery; the two girls lying silently together as friends. It was then, late at night, that I decided to write the 'Babes in the Wood' case in its entirety and to leave aside for the time being all thought of investigating other crimes.

A Question of Evidence sets out to explain, and indeed attempts to solve, two brutal cases of murder for which a young man, Russell Bishop, was arrested, arraigned and then freed as 'Not Guilty'. Throughout the daunting research I have, I hope, acted objectively and honestly. I have been, in addition, severely restricted by understandable legal restraints from voicing my suspicions. I was assisted by a large number of individuals, including the Hadaways, Fellows and Bishop families, who in their deep grief nonetheless offered me hospitality and much needed background advice. Russell Bishop, who spent over a year in custody, helped where he could; this in itself makes *A Question of Evidence* unique. As a direct result of my research, all families joined together in an attempt to have the case re-opened.

The Sussex Constabulary were not able to associate themselves in any way with my compilation of facts, therefore I had to rely very much on my own wits throughout the project. I am very sad, too, that other individuals who had it in their power to help did not come forward, despite repeated requests. This raises serious questions which are aired in the pages that follow. What I am able to say is that when work for *A Question of Evidence* began, the police were not pursuing their enquiries into these two murders. Having failed to convict Russell Bishop, their attitude seemed to be that 'a killer had got away'. However, when new facts were raised by my research, fresh evidence was presented to Detective Superintendent Christopher Page, Deputy Head of Sussex CID, as a result of which the Sussex police interviewed new witnesses. The people of Brighton took a fresh initiative, too, and after a public demonstration and considerable media coverage, the Sussex police for a short period did take a new line: 'The case is very much open again and will remain so until the killer is brought to justice.'

On Friday, 14 December 1990 the tabloid headlines shouted 'Justice For Our Babes' and 'I Know He Killed Karen'. Twenty-four-year-old Russell Bishop had been convicted at Lewes Crown Court the previous day on various charges including the attempted murder of a young girl. The resentment felt by Brighton people since Bishop had been cleared of murdering Karen Hadaway and Nicola Fellows in 1986 erupted in court. As the tearful father of three was led down to the cells after Mr Justice Nolan jailed him for life, there were cheers and shouts of

'He should hang!' Crowds had jostled for places in the public gallery at Lewes Crown Court during the three-week trial and now they eagerly scanned the papers for confirmation of their views. The early editions of the *Evening Argus* were filled with the day's events in court. Said one regular attender, it was 'the biggest show on earth'.

Despite his conviction for an entirely different crime, the newspapers had decided that Bishop was guilty of the Babes in the Wood murders and in saying so in bold print they completely overruled the English criminal justice system which had already acquitted him. There were no protests, just an expression of relief that a kind of rough justice had been enacted by newsprint. The police now told reporters, 'We have no plans to re-open enquiries . . . we are not looking for anyone else.'

The fact remains that the Babes in the Wood murders remain unsolved. Apart from accusation based on prejudice, no evidence has been brought forward since his acquittal to prove that the Wild Park killings were committed by Bishop.

It was inevitable that his conviction would recall the earlier murders, and his previous trial: it would be expecting too much of human nature for it to be otherwise. This time a number of participants who had had their reputations dented in 1986 could redeem themselves and the police could gloss over their past shortcomings and say that the matter was at last closed. On the face of it, the only person to suffer, apart from the girls' anguished parents, was Russell Bishop, and since he had now been found guilty of a brutal sexual assault on a child, why waste any sympathy on him?

A Question of Evidence does not challenge the correctness of the court's verdict on Bishop in December 1990;

indeed, that decision is irrelevant as far as the Babes in the Wood enquiry is concerned, and certainly does not close the file.

Eight years almost to the day before the deaths of Karen and Nicola, again on a cold October night, a young, vivacious mother, Margaret Frame, aged thirty-four, was walking her dog through Stanmer Park in Brighton. On her way towards Coldean Lane she was struck a violent blow, stabbed through the heart and brutally raped. Her cold body was discovered in a shallow grave less than half a mile from the spot where the Babes in the Wood were found. Despite extensive enquiries by the Sussex police, her killer has not been arrested and brought to justice, nor is the file closed.

Any unsolved murder enquiry poses questions of public safety and for the sake of the public good demands attention. All those who are so ready to close the Babes in the Wood file might stop to think about some of the questions raised here. What if, despite the newspapers' blaring headlines, Bishop did not commit the Wild Park killings? What if someone else was involved, separately or with his knowledge? What if evidence had been mishandled, misinterpreted? What if the wrong questions were asked? What if the murderer is still at large?

1. The Moulsecoomb Families

Karen Hadaway and Nicola Fellows were found dead in a densely wooded area some two miles north of Brighton's town centre at 4.21 p.m. on the afternoon of Friday, 10 October 1986. Both had been strangled, both had been sexually assaulted, Karen before she died and Nicola twice, after death. They had been seen at 6.45 p.m. the previous evening, playing happily together a mere few hundred yards from their Moulsecoomb council homes. Now they lay as if asleep, tucked up in the dark, tangled undergrowth that formed a natural 'den'.

Over a hundred concerned individuals had been searching for them throughout the long, misty night; during the next day the numbers had swelled enormously. Like a spinning wheel off-balance, Brighton's busy centre uncomfortably shifted ground. Radio and television drew people to the search, now focused on the 190 acres of almost rugged downland known as the Wild Park, quite close to Moulsecoomb. Fear and confusion, coupled with great public concern, emanated from the council estate. Two little schoolgirls had gone missing from their homes. The urgent message was: 'Keep an eye open for these young children.' It reached every inhabitant of Brighton, it reached neighbouring towns and villages. Panic and suspicion threatened to engulf this outwardly respectable community. The murders of Karen and Nicola were about to rip away the warm, secure mantle that had wrapped Brighton round since its halcyon days of Regency glory that earned it the appellation 'A Royal Retreat'.

The very name Brighton could hardly have been improved on, indeed its smart, glittering sound makes it seem modern, a name coined for a sophisticated pleasure resort. In fact, it dates from 1810, when the Town Commissioners dropped the old name, Brightelmstone, that had been in use as early as 1660, in the reign of King Charles II, along with 40 or 50 variants like Brighthelmstead and Bright-Hampstead. Records of the area's first inhabitants date back to a tribal occupation by Continental immigrants around 2700 BC. In the Domesday Book it is called Bristlmestune.

Another name emerges from Duke William's survey, that of Moulsecoomb, the district that today spreads along the north-eastern side of the Brighton to Lewes Road and up on to the edge of the South Downs. This name is apparently derived from 'Mul', King of the Saxons, who was burnt in the neighbourhood by avenging Kentish warriors angered by his laying waste their country. 'Coombe' is the ancient term for valley. Alternative spellings down the years have included Molstan (in the Domesday Book) and also Molecumbe, Mulscombe and Moulscomb. It was only in 1957 that the present spelling of Moulsecoomb was agreed upon. Until the creation of the present residential estates, the land was mainly used for farming, the only really significant building being Moulsecoomb Place; built in 1350, it was once a favourite haunt of the Prince Regent.

Brighton's development as a resort – a watering place – began when bathing became fashionable in the mid-eighteenth century. Floyer and Edward Baynard, two

London medical practitioners, published praises of the cures effected by sea-water bathing: asthma, cancer, consumption, deafness, ruptures, rheumatism and madness were just some of the diseases and ailments it could banish. Carried away with enthusiasm, the distinguished authors burst into verse:

> Cold bathing has this cure alone:
> It makes old John to hug old Joan;
> And does fresh kindness entail
> On a wife tasteless, old and stale.

The prospect of renewed sexual vitality has always been the surest guarantee of any cure's success. 'Bathing machines' were introduced in 1735, and by the 1770s, Brighton attracted numbers of visitors, becoming the scene of great balls and assemblies once the seasonal residency of the Prince of Wales had conferred the Royal seal of approval. By the 1920s, the glories had dimmed. Brighton was run down and the depression inflicted still more problems.

Between 1920 and 1931, though, the town's Corporation cleared the old slum houses in the lower part of the Sussex Street and Carlton Hill area, steep streets leading eastwards from the Steyne and Grand Parade. Running parallel with Corporation developments were a considerable number of commercial undertakings. Property speculators moved in, notably at Patcham, Ovingdean, Woodingdean and Rottingdean, all on the outskirts of the borough. Crime was rife and protection racketeers prospered by intimidating luckless publicans and café proprietors. Hordes of pick-pockets, thieves, sharks, tricksters, pimps and harlots swarmed to the resort like so many carrion, intent on feeding off the rich, vulnerable pickings to be had, while most of the visitors walking the freshly scrubbed streets remained blissfully ignorant of their predations. Then Brighton's unsavoury reputation as a haunt of crime and violence was dramatically exposed by a succession of four grisly murders; three of them, including the two notorious Brighton trunk murders, occurred during a single year. The town was referred to, somewhat cruelly, as 'The Queen of Slaughtering Places'.

The slum dwellers had been resettled in new housing estates at Moulsecoomb, Whitehawk and Manor Farm, all to the east of Brighton. The general standards of design and layout of the houses were far below those of the municipally planned estates, but at least the Moulsecoomb architects, breaking away from the long-established layout of council estates, with homes crammed in long lines into confined areas, built their estates with imagination and with considerable consideration for the landscape. South Moulsecoomb was started in 1921, North Moulsecoomb in 1926 and, finally, East Moulsecoomb in the early 1930s. Their houses and streets seemed to flow into and around the hills and meadows, but the Utopia that was to be Moulsecoomb fell drastically short of the Corporation's desires. Within a generation, North Moulsecoomb in particular had gained the reputation as a dumping ground for problem families. People who had experienced long periods of unemployment and hardship were seemingly judged by the Corporation's Housing Department as unfit to live in Brighton's sparkling town centre and were shuffled to the Moulsecoomb estates where higher rents, 22 shillings a week compared with 15 shillings in the town centre, simply exacerbated their problems. Used to town life, they felt isolated on the Downs, and turned in upon themselves and their community. The criminal element grew and flourished and by the 1970s Moulsecoomb had become a 'twilight district', even, according to one researcher, a 'no go' area where police feared to tread. In fact there were so many public and domestic disturbances there that the Sussex Constabulary invested funds in a manned police post located on the Brighton to Lewes Road, at the edge of the Wild Park.

Some 7000 residents are packed into an area for parts of which the description 'run down' would seem an understatement. A video shown by the local housing pressure group in 1985 graphically portrayed electric sockets hanging from walls by dangerous wiring, ceilings and walls black with mould and damp, the wallpaper peeling. The damp had caused food tins to go rusty in kitchens; clothes, furniture and bedding were stained with green mould. Some of the houses were described as wind tunnels by virtue of their badly fitted doors and windows; in most, the kitchens were too small and some still had the old chipped stone sinks. Many houses had just one coal fire for heating. The exterior of many buildings echoed their interior condition: rotting timbers and paintwork, dripping gutters, broken windows boarded up with cardboard and tape. Gardens, their turf scoured to bare earth, were crammed with rusty cycles and broken pushchairs; many residents could not remove large items of rubbish to the nearby tip because they had no means of transport. Steps leading to homes were in a dangerous condition and there were no garden fences to prevent children from running into the busy, badly lit roads where untaxed, clapped-out motor vehicles stood jacked up on bricks awaiting repairs that would never be afforded. Dogs roamed the streets, unlicensed, uncollared and often unwanted, fouling gardens and pavements.

One resident told me: 'Moulsecoomb had got a reputation

as a slum where all the roughs go and there is a lot of
violence. I don't blame the people who say that, because it
is. It's a pretty rough area to look at.' This contrasts with
the view of another resident, Mrs Sylvia Folkes of
Southall Avenue, who is fiercely proud of her community: 'I may have to go to Brighton for my bingo, but I
would not want to move out of here.'

The last few years have seen some improvement, in the
form of new homes. Many residents keep well-groomed
gardens, with neat privet hedges; clean, crisp net curtains
in stark contrast with a neighbour's filthy windows. Pro-
ceeding south, signs of greater affluence grow, with the
appearance of cars of more recent vintage. But it was into
the unimproved world of crammed deprivation at North
Moulsecoomb that Karen Hadaway and Nicola Fellows
were born.

Standing near ancient Hollingbury Castle, a mere stone's
throw from the Ditchling Road, it is possible to look across
a part of the Wild park known locally as the 'Giant's Foot'
and gaze upon the North Moulsecoomb estate and the
expanse of Falmer Hill lying to the east. From a distance
everything seems pleasant and peaceful. Murmurs of con-
versations are carried on the breeze from the nearby Hollingbury golf course. The sweet smell of pine and freshly
mown grass pervades the air and, on sunny days, hundreds of people enjoy the delight of ambling through the
lush green valley. The Wild Park is ringed with trees and
undergrowth. In springtime, bluebells grow in the shade;
later on, buttercups brighten the grass with their glow.

Newick Road in the North Moulsecoomb estate was
home to the Babes in the Wood. Michelle Lesley Hadaway
née Johnson was born 7 January 1957. She married Lee
Michael Hadaway on 17 August 1974. They lived with

Michelle's grandparents in Ditchling Road, Brighton, and on 29 November that year their first child was born, a son whom they named Darren. They moved to Lavender Street, a mere quarter of a mile from the beach and Brighton's Marine Parade, then in 1976 the family were re-housed by the council and moved to 47 Birdham Road, Moulsecoomb. Shortly after they had settled into their new address, Karen Jane Michelle was born on 21 December 1976, almost a Christmas baby. A second daughter, Lyndsey Kelly Michelle, was born on 21 January 1981.

While they were living at Birdham Road the Hadaways suffered their first tragedy. Darren had a serious fall from a bedroom window, suffering injuries that caused behavioural problems which in turn resulted in learning difficulties. He was attending Moulsecoomb School at the time but was moved to St John's Residential School in Walpole Road, Brighton, boarding during the week but returning home at weekends and during school holidays. In 1982 the Hadaways moved to 20 Newick Road, Moulsecoomb; two years later, in June 1984, Michelle's mother, Maisie Johnson, moved in with them, following the death of her husband.

Lee Hadaway is a quiet, unassuming man who does not tolerate fools gladly. Born on 16 September 1948, he stands just under six feet and speaks little except when he has enjoyed his favourite tipple, a glass or more of Scotch. He had regular employment as a builder's labourer until 1985, but gave up his job because it meant living away from home so much; the Hadaways are a close-knit family. Both parents are always able to express their love for their children, whom they adore. They struggle to maintain a good standard of life for their family in a difficult environment. It might be said that they were almost over-protective. Obviously they couldn't keep the children at home all day if they were to lead a normal, healthy life, but when the kiddies went out to play it was usually close to home or at places known to their parents.

Both Lee and Michelle cooperated in every possible way with the compilation of this book. At times it broke their hearts.

Susan Patricia Fellows *née* Streeter was born on 19 September 1949; two days later, on 21 September, Barrie John Fellows entered this world. They married on 19 September 1970 at St George's Church, Kemp Town, Brighton and lived at that time at 22 Rudwick Road, Hollingbury. Their first child, born on 7 December 1971, was a boy, Jonathan Barrie. On 22 February 1977 they had a daughter, Nicola Elizabeth Christine. The Fellows family moved to 26 Newick Road in 1980, sharing their home with Susan's mother, Mabel Edna Victoria Streeter. Like Mrs Johnson at the Hadaways, she was a widow.

Barrie had a reputation on the Moulsecoomb Estate as a hard man. As a youth he had led a life of petty crime which landed him in jail; he was convicted at various times of deception, burglary and receiving stolen goods. He has three brothers; Nigel, Ian and Kevin. Ian is a serving police constable with the Essex Constabulary. Kevin is a large, hard, no-nonsense individual capable of lifting twice his own weight; he holds down various jobs. Nigel issues a business card which declares him to be a private investigator.

After some initial reluctance to assist with this book, all four brothers finally consented to help, providing most of the documentary material without which it could not have been written. Nigel and Kevin in particular spent many hours with me; their companionship was invaluable. Susan Fellows did not speak more than a few words to me.

In 1985, Douglas Simon Judd moved in with the Fellows; he had known them for eight years. The introduction into Britain of Citizens' Band Radio (CB) was responsible for bringing Barrie and Douggie together. They were both radio 'hams' and chatted together over the airwaves. Judd's call-sign or 'handle', as it is known among enthusiasts, was either 'Sud Soaps' or 'Pain Killer'; Fellows' was 'Basil Brush'. Both men would sit in parked cars sporting oversize aerials at high, isolated spots, talking to each other and to anyone else on the wave band.

Born on 1 September 1964, Douglas Judd belonged to a family of four boys and two girls. Douglas did not get on well with his mother and left home to live with the Fellows. Nicola shared a room with her grandmother; they had separate beds. Jonathan had his own room, as did Barrie and Susan. Douggie slept in a ground-floor room for which he paid £25 a week. He was unemployed. In October 1986 he enjoyed the company of a fifteen-year-old girl named Jackie, who lived in Ashurst Road, Moulsecoomb.

Russell Bishop, another local man, was born on 9 February 1966. His father, Roy, was a roofer and his mother, Sylvia, a successful international dog trainer; her book *It's Magic*, a complete manual and step-by-step guide to dog training, is a bestseller. Russell has four brothers: Alec, David, Andrew and Michael. He went to Coldean School, where the staff realised he had learning and behaviour problems; he was found to be partially dyslexic. He was sent to a special Catholic school in Worcester, then returned to Sussex to attend St Mary's day and residential school in Horah Road, near Heathfield. Unable to settle as a boarder, he took to running away, hitch-hiking to

Brighton to be near his family. He was taken away from St
Mary's and, from the age of sixteen, was given a private
education by a family friend, Mrs Angela Saunders.

Bishop knew both the Fellows and the Hadaway families. He was also a CB user; so was his common-law wife,
Jennie Johnson – their handles were 'Silver Bullet' and
'Panda Bear'. They lived together at 17 Stephen's Road in
the Hollingdean Estate. Bishop had a girlfriend, too:
Marion Stevenson, who lived in Barcombe Road in Moulsecoomb. He spent some of his time doing up cars, his own
and other people's. He had two Fords, an Escort and a
Cortina.

It seemed that all three households were set in that ever-
downward spiral of humdrum domestic life which offered
nothing more than a daily routine of cooking, cleaning,
odd-jobbing, looking after the children and making the
occasional foray to local shops. A visit to what was then
the Labour Exchange, now called the Job Centre, gave the
men a bus ride into Brighton now and then in order to
sign on. The women were content to drift in and out of
each other's homes to gossip the hours away.

It would be correct to say that both Karen and Nicola
enjoyed their schooling. Karen attended Coldean Junior
School, Selham Drive, Coldean. Her teacher, Andrew
David Wilson, who had taught there for some five years,
described her to the police as a lively, cheerful but not
very bright child. She mixed well with the other children
in the class and was very close to her friend Claire Shepherd – she went to Claire's tenth birthday party the day
before she disappeared.

Karen normally left home in the morning around 8.20
a.m. A number 25 bus service stopped at the bottom of
Coldean Lane, outside the school. Karen simply walked

into Lewes Road, under the subway, and waited for her bus. It was safe enough and she generally escorted her younger sister Lyndsey. The return journey in the afternoon was the same trip in reverse. If Karen walked to school, she was taken by her mother on almost every occasion.

Moulsecoomb Middle School provided Nicola with her education, just under a mile from her home. Her teacher was Donald Rees, who had taught there since 1977. On 2 September 1986 the autumn term started and Mr Rees became form teacher for Class 39's 24 children, one of whom was Nicola. In fact she did not attend school for the first week of term because there was some doubt whether or not she would attend that or another school in the catchment area. On Monday, 8 September, Nicola and her father went to Moulsecoomb Middle School and the headmaster, Allen Nathan Roochove, took them to see Mr Rees. There had been a problem during previous terms: Nicola had been caught taking items not belonging to her. Her school report indicated that she was a slow learner and it was recommended that she received special tuition during morning lessons in the Unit Class taken by Mr Rob Stone. She attended school regularly after this, missing only one and a half days until she died: she had developed an eye infection and missed the afternoon session on 25 September and all the following day.

Donald Rees' report depicted Nicola as a happy, friendly, outgoing child who caused no problems in the classroom. She was in apparent good health, showing no signs of bruising or any other injuries which might indicate something other than a decent home life. But this report was contradicted by Mr Roochove's. He described Nicola as a difficult child who was socially badly adjusted. Her work was poor, she was sullen and spiteful and had no friends at school. On a number of occasions since his appointment in January 1986 he had had reason to call at the Fellows' home to complain about the theft of small items by Nicola, and on that Monday, 8 September, Barrie Fellows had placed a number of items on Mr Roochove's desk and said that as far as he was concerned the issue was now closed. Nicola would not steal again.

In a confidential document – a police statement – leaked to me, Roochove alleges that Fellows took hold of Nicola's right hand and said, 'If she does it again she knows what I will do: cut them off.' Roochove interjected that Fellows would not cut off his daughter's fingers and readily enough Fellows agreed. But the headmaster formed the professional opinion that Nicola was a very nervous girl. Her fingernails were bitten right down, she twitched and blinked a lot, and in her father's company these traits were more pronounced.

2. Home from School

The morning of 9 October 1986 dawned with a grey wet mist struggling to lift itself off the Moulsecoomb Estate. Nicola had been woken by her mother, shouting upstairs as all parents do, in an attempt to raise a child from a warm bed. She got up and slipped on a pair of long white socks and a pair of bright red shoes, which her mother had bought at the Sunday market held at Brighton's railway station each week. She took a pair of clean white knickers from a drawer, bought from 'Primark' at the beginning of the school holidays; her skirt, a brown and cream tartan pattern, had been found in a second-hand shop in London Road. A pink sweatshirt completed her outfit for the day. She always wore a fresh set of clothes each day for school, well washed in Daz. She ate two slices of toast and then, according to her mother's statement, dated 15 October 1986, she left for school at 8.15 a.m. Her grandmother, Edna, says the time was more like 8.20 a.m.

Karen Hadaway dressed herself in her school uniform. Over her white underwear she pulled on a grey pleated skirt, a blue T-shirt and the green Coldean School sweater. She chose white knee-length socks and a pair of pink trainers. She ate a light breakfast, too; there was always a selection of cereals in the larder. Then, with 73 pence in her pocket, she set off to catch her bus, leaving home at 8.10 a.m.

Both girls arrived at their respective schools without incident. After school assembly, Nicola went swimming with the rest of her class at the King Alfred Baths in Brighton, then spent the rest of the morning in class. When the morning session finished at 12.40 a.m. she remained at school and enjoyed school dinner with her pals. At 1.20 p.m. she returned to her classroom and stayed there until school finished at 2.45 p.m. She attended extra choir practice and made her own way home, arriving at about 3.45 p.m.

Karen finished classes at 3.15 p.m. and walked down to the bus stop with four schoolfriends: Lisa Huggins, Claire Shepherd, Kelly Muggeridge and Sarah Windsor. For some reason Sarah became the subject of a little joke: the girls began to tease her because she wouldn't carry Claire's money. Karen apparently punched Sarah, then wandered off with Claire and Kelly. She arrived safely home at 4.05 p.m. She had missed the first bus, but that was not unusual.

Their families imposed a strict schedule on the children's journeys to and from school: a police letter had been circulated to all parents of local children explaining that during the previous fortnight a ginger-haired man driving a blue car had been seen prowling round schools in the Sussex area; several children had complained that a man in his twenties had tried to entice them into his car, at Lewes, Newick and Rottingdean. On each occasion the child had refused. Police made several visits to schools to warn children of the danger and even issued a special warning in the form of an appeal for information printed in the *Evening Argus*.

Several schoolgirls had spotted a ginger-haired man sitting in a car either red or blue – their memory was vague over the colour, but neon street lamps can drastically alter colours – which sported a dark roof. One child maintained that at about 6 p.m. on 9 October she had seen a man dragging Karen into a vehicle near the cricket pavilion in the Wild Park and gave a description of a red car with a black roof. Another child, out buying fish and chips, saw a man, dirty in appearance, sitting in a dark blue or red Cortina parked at the kerbside. There were *two* men inside the car, but the one that captured the girl's attention had curly ginger or fair hair; the other wore dark glasses. A similar sighting was made around the same time but at a different location – opposite the police box in Lewes Road: two men were seen in a parked car eating what appeared to be fish and chips; one man wore dark glasses and the other a black leather jacket.

These accounts of *two* men sitting in either a red or dark blue Ford Cortina are significant. Each reported one man apparently in his twenties with fair or ginger hair, the other wearing dark glasses. Both sightings were at locations where Karen and Nicola were seen that evening by other witnesses: Karen had been seen near a fish and chip shop in Coldean Lane and both girls had passed another fish and chip shop on their way out to play after school.

Lee Hadaway was away from home on 9 October: he had joined Stephen Judd, Douggie's brother, who was on a business trip to the Midlands. Stephen was unemployed but he held a Heavy Goods Vehicle driving licence and with it was able to find occasional employment as a lorry driver. One of the companies that employed him was Leospeed Limited, of Lewes in Sussex, removal and delivery contractors who specialise in the transit of furniture throughout Britain. The company declined an invitation to assist with the research for this book.

On the morning of Wednesday, 8 October Stephen

Judd had telephoned Leospeed, who informed him that they had a Mercedes lorry laden with furniture to be delivered to various locations throughout the Midlands. Judd collected the vehicle at 11.30 a.m. on 8 October, obtaining his route instructions from David Otterway, an employee of Leospeed. The deliveries were to take him to Cambridge, Birmingham, Great Glen near Birmingham, and a small town in Norfolk; on the return journey he was to make deliveries at other places in the Manchester area. On previous trips he had been accompanied by Barrie Fellows, but on this occasion he knew Fellows had found work cleaning out a swimming pool at an address in Hove. Feeling the need for company, and assistance in moving heavy items of furniture, he asked if Lee Hadaway would come, and he agreed. Before leaving, Lee called on Douggie Judd to ask if he would wander out later that day, or during the evening, to collect a few extra names for his window-cleaning round. This Judd agreed to do.

Stephen Judd and Lee Hadaway left Moulsecoomb at midday and set off for Cambridge; but Judd drove down to the West Country, making for Cambridge near Gloucester, although his route instructions clearly specified Cambridge in Cambridgeshire. The two men arrived at their erroneous destination around 4 p.m. Realising their mistake, they sped off for Cambridge proper, arriving at 10.15 p.m. They stopped travelling at 11 p.m. because the vehicle's tachograph prevented them driving any further that day, and slept in the back of the lorry. The following morning they set off again in earnest to make their overdue deliveries. Their first call was at 8.30 a.m.

On returning home from school on 9 October, Nicola had gone straight to her bedroom, removed her long white socks and replaced the red shoes. She was still at home

when she heard a knock at the front door. Michelle Hadaway, well into her fourth pregnancy, was visiting Susan
Fellows at the time and she recalled Nicola opening the
door to two young women, Tracey Anne Cox and Marion
Stevenson, and to Russell Bishop. Bishop asked if Douggie
Judd was at home, and realising that Judd was still at
work or on his way home, Nicola replied rudely, 'No, he's
not,' and slammed the door. As the threesome trailed
back into Newick Road, she shouted through the broken
letterbox, 'Go away, you slag.'

This remark was directed towards Marion Stevenson.
Bishop had been enjoying what the tabloid press term a
steamy relationship with her; and Nicola, in the
knowledge that Bishop's common-law wife, Jennie
Johnson, was heavily pregnant with his child, resented
this. Bishop laughed at the catcall and both women giggled. They separated, Bishop turning left and the two
young women right. Bishop had another call to make
that evening, one he could not miss. He was off to steal a
car and then buy drugs from a friend, expecting to meet
Marion later at her home, at 6.30 p.m. He did not turn
up.

Michelle Hadaway left the Fellows' house and walked
home to find Karen extremely excited and waving a disco
ticket. 'Mum, Mum, it's my school disco, I can go, can't I?
she pleaded. She had every reason to be excited. It was her
first dance. She felt grown up and very important. Karen
went on to tell her mother that Claire, her schoolfriend,
had given her ten pence. She asked if she could walk up to
the Wavy Line shop, called H. A. Wrights, in Coldean, to
buy a 'Tip Top' drink. She discarded her jacket and her
mother told her to change out of school uniform. She
disobeyed and went straight out to play, leaving Michelle
Hadaway to prepare a chicken pie dinner. The last words

Karen spoke to her mother were: 'I'm off now.' The front door opened and closed.

At approximately 4.40 p.m. Karen joined her sister Lyndsey playing in the street. Philip Reeve, a self-employed painter and decorator, had just finished work for the day; he was sub-contracted to B. J. Blatcher of Seaford, who were developing a new housing site at the north end of Newick Road. He had parked his green Morris 1000 outside 18 Newick Road. As he approached, Karen spoke to him from her front garden. She was tucking into a packet of Smith's crisps. 'I've been sitting on your car,' she volunteered. Reeve replied, 'You mustn't do that, you'll dent it,' to which she retorted, 'I'm not that fat!' She told him that she had been sitting on the front wing and went on to say that her nanny was a 'pig' because she wouldn't let her have any of her crisps. Reeve drove off in his car at 4.45 p.m.

From there Karen went to play in the garden of 15 Newick Road. Mrs Sharon Julie Bowles was in bed and heard shouting from her front garden. She estimated the time at around 4.45 p.m. and noted that Karen was playing with her sister Lyndsey, Nicola Fellows and several other children including her own, Simon, Philip and Lisa. She saw Karen give Lyndsey a 'dig' in the back; Lyndsey wanted a roller boot that the other children were playing with and wouldn't let her have. Minutes later Mrs Bowles watched as Nicola and Karen ran off down Newick Road towards Barcombe Road. They were laughing.

Very soon after, both girls were spotted by Mrs Elizabeth Chapman. She had been running to catch a number 28 bus that would take her into Brighton where she worked as a cleaner for American Express, and as she arrived at the bus stop she saw Nicola and Karen doing cartwheels on the pavement of Barcombe Road. A number of other people saw the girls. One of these was Roy Victor Dadswell, a uniformed Park Constable working for the Brighton Corporation. His duties involved patrolling and supervising the Wild Park, and at 5.15 p.m. he noticed Karen and Nicola swinging rather dangerously on the branch of a tree near the park entrance. Wisely, he asked them to get down. They giggled and ran off.

As the clock on Michelle Hadaway's wall moved to 5.30 p.m., Karen was still not home. The chicken pie was getting cold; darkness and mist were settling over the house.

At 5.45 p.m., Alan Vickery, on his way to 18 Park Road to collect an electric drill, was held up at the traffic lights at the junction of Coldean Lane and Lewes Road. He noticed two girls sitting on the wall of the pedestrian subway. When he drove home some ten minutes later, he saw the girls were still there.

At 6.20 p.m. they were seen outside a fish and chip shop in Park Road by Mrs Green, who was with her daughter. Five minutes later they were seen again, apparently eating fish and chips, near the entrance to the Wild Park.

There were perhaps three other sightings worth mentioning. One came from a schoolgirl who had been out delivering newspapers. She also saw the girls at about 6.20 p.m. She recalled what they were wearing and remembered a snippet of conversation Nicola was having with Karen. Nicola told this young witness that she and Karen were going into the Wild Park. The newspaper girl said that they shouldn't – their mothers would be worried because it was getting late. Nicola ignored her and shouted to Karen, 'Come on, let's go into the park!' Karen replied that she wasn't interested, that she might go in a minute.

During a subsequent BBC *Crimewatch* programme the

police screened a request for witnesses to come forward. Among the viewers was Kevin James Carhart, owner of a hairdressing shop in Duke Street, Brighton. He recalled that he had seen two young girls darting across the busy Lewes Road at about 6.40 p.m. and that he had braked to avoid hitting them. He had also noticed two men on the central reservation, heading towards the girls. The third sighting was reported by Mrs Northcliffe, exercising her black labrador, Beauty, and black-and-tan German Shepherd, Nicki. This witness remembered one of the girls in every detail, remarking on a very pretty face with a lovely smile. This girl, she said, wore a light-coloured top which in the orange glow of the street lamps looked very light. She had described Nicola Fellows to a tee.

Karen and Nicola were never seen alive again.

3. The Search

The normal procedure during the early stages of a 'Missing Persons' case does not involve a vast deployment of police manpower. The Babes in the Wood case was to be an exception, though, for by 11.00 p.m. on 9 October over a hundred officers had been drafted into the area. Police searched the local schools. Karen's headmistress, Mrs Mary Stenton, was woken by a loud banging on her front door. She recalled saying that Lee Hadaway had often gone fishing, that Michelle Hadaway had told her Karen sometimes accompanied him. All Mrs Stenton's staff were contacted through the night. Dozens of police and neighbours walked through the woods and parkland. They searched gardens and outhouses. Douggie Judd borrowed a pal's bicycle, then called at the home of another friend, another CB radio enthusiast. This man, call-sign 'Hair Bear', put out a 1033 emergency call asking for fellow receivers to look out for the two girls. Almost immediately the call was returned with a spine-chilling message: 'This is Whispering Willie. I've killed the girls.' The caller's handset was replaced, slammed down.

Other CB users sprang into action. Setting up a 'control base', they first cleared their search intentions with the Sussex police. A number of men clambered into a blue Transit van owned by 26-year-old Yann Svenski and sped off to the Bate's Estate area of Patcham. A few men were dropped off there and the van was parked at Moul-secoomb railway station. The time was just before 12.45 a.m. on Friday, 10 October. Using powerful torches, Philip Upton, Simon Barnes and Yann Svenski searched an area separating the platforms from a dead-end track.

Suddenly someone ran through the bushes, setting the hairs on Svenski's neck tingling in fright. He called out to his friends and, reassured by their replies, resumed his search. Minutes later, they discovered a pale blue sweatshirt on the damp grass. The garment was inside out and it was also bone dry, giving the distinct impression that it had been recently discarded. It smelt of body odour and carried the legend 'Pinto' emblazoned in white on the front. They radioed in, saying that the size was approximately a 40-inch chest. The police returned their call, saying that neither girl had been wearing that item. Svenski left it draped over a metal railing fence, totally unaware that the girls' killer had missed him by just a few black yards.

By morning a massive search was under way. More than 150 uniformed officers and 30 detectives joined frantic relatives and friends to search streets and parks for the youngsters. The Schools' Police Liaison Officer started to speak to children at Coldean Middle School in case any child could throw light on the mystery. Officers began the laborious task of knocking on every door in the area. Every householder was requested to search their gardens and outbuildings. A police helicopter clattered overhead. It was equipped with a thermal imaging device and began a 'box search' of the area: flying a specific grid pattern over the park and nearby estates.

At 10.30 a.m. a rendezvous point was set up at Moul-secoomb police box on Lewes Road. Police Superin-tendent David Tomlinson had assumed overall charge of an operation that was to demand more police manpower and resources than the 1984 IRA bombing of the Conservative Party Conference at Brighton's Grand Hotel. He initiated a search of the railway line and ordered police tracker dogs into the nearby woods and fields. Just after lunch he issued a statement to gathering reporters: 'We are desperately concerned for the welfare of these children,' he said.

Nicola's head teacher at Moulsecoomb Middle School also made a statement to the press: 'The response from the school and the community has been fantastic. Moulsecoomb has a terrible reputation which it doesn't deserve, and it is at times like this, when something terrible happens, that you see it in its true spirit.' There can be no doubt that Mr Roochove meant well and certainly the community did, in the main, respond magnificently. But as the tragedy began to unfold, so the truly evil side of Moulsecoomb began to manifest itself.

Lee Hadaway had learned of his daughter's absence from home when he telephoned his wife at 5.45 p.m. on the evening of 9 October. He promised to call every half-hour, which he did. Michelle Hadaway wandered into Brighton and, standing on the deserted beach, called out her daughter's name a thousand times. The roar of crashing surf, dragging well-worn pebbles down into a cold sea, swept her cries away unanswered on the night wind. Her husband had later spoken to the police and they asked him to return to Brighton, where he was to arrive the next day. He discussed the situation with Stephen Judd, who still had more deliveries to make the following day. Lee was not insured to travel in the lorry and Leospeed had in fact forbidden Judd to use anyone to assist on deliveries. Judd could give no acceptable excuse for failing to deliver

the remainder of the furniture. He telephoned the
Brighton police, who ordered him to find a police station,
get his tachograph signed by a senior officer, then proceed
straight back to Brighton with Lee.

Barrie Fellows and Douggie Judd apparently arrived
home from work around 7.30 p.m. on the 9th. Both men
made a number of statements to the police, each changing
considerably with regard to times and places. What Douggie Judd is sure of is that he telephoned the police to
report that the girls were missing at about 7.30 p.m. after
he had eaten his tea, and that Barrie Fellows arrived home
shortly after this telephone call had been made. The
Sussex police were apparently happy to accept this
account without question. It has now been accepted by
the police that only one telephone call was made that
evening to report the girls missing, a fact confirmed in a
document I discovered. However, there is one crucial
difference in that information supplied by it.

Ester Erika O'Connell is a woman police officer based at
John Street police station in Brighton. Her duties for 9
October 1986 included a spell in the Communications
Room. In her statement dated 17 October 1986, she says:
'At 20.36 hrs on Thursday, 9 October 1986, whilst on duty
in the Communications Room, Police Station, Brighton, I
received a phone call from a male caller reporting a Nicola
Fellows and Karen Hadaway as missing children. This
conversation was recorded on tape 59 and I produce this
tape as Exhibit EEO/1.' An 'Area Car' was despatched to
Moulsecoomb and several other officers were ordered by
radio to proceed at once to Newick Road to obtain a full
description of the children.

This was the call made by Douglas Judd. Barrie Fellows
arrived home after that call was made, more than an hour
later than he claimed. There were also discrepancies in the

two men's accounts of their movements that day. They claimed that they worked together cleaning out a swimming pool in Hove, then caught a bus home. I interviewed two of their workmates and learned that one of these men gave Judd a lift home in his car, dropping him off at Moulsecoomb at about 5.30 p.m. Another workmate of Fellows and Judd, the contractor who employed them both, was interviewed by me and by Barrie Fellows' brother, Nigel Heffron. This man claimed that as he and his wife and daughter were sitting down to dinner on 9 October, they received a telephone call from a concerned Barrie Fellows claiming that Nicola was missing, and requesting that the contractor get his car out to help in the search. This call was received at around 6.55 p.m., at least half an hour before Fellows, by his own statement, had learned of his daughter's disappearance. When these and other matters were put to the Brighton police, Detective Chief Superintendent Chris Page laughed them off, saying, 'One cannot trust any of the times, as most of the people of Moulsecoomb cannot even afford to own a watch.' It is interesting to note that Barrie Fellows and Douglas Judd were later treated as suspects in this case, although the Brighton police did not feel it necessary to interview their workmates for that day. That was left to me. However, both men were later eliminated from police enquiries.

On his arrival home from work, Barrie Fellows had sat down for his dinner, later assisting the police in their desperate search. He had been issued with a flashlight. Stumbling over the wet grass, he explored the area in the Wild Park adjacent to the old cricket pavilion. He passed the toilets but omitted to look behind the building: in the past he had told Nicola not to go near because a 'Boogie Man' lived there. The children were found dead a mere 30 yards away. Fellows returned home just after 10.00 p.m. to snap at his wife, 'Why the bleedin' hell did you let her bloody well out?' She tried to reply but he cut her short. 'If anything has happened by my little Nicky, I'll kill the bastards.' He went to bed.

Russell Bishop came into the reckoning during the afternoon of the 10th. At about 2.30 p.m. he wandered up to Marion Stevenson, standing gossiping at the police box opposite the Moulsecoomb Estate. He was carrying an item of clothing belonging to Karen, given to him by Michelle Hadaway with police permission. Bishop's mother owned a tracker dog called Misty and, as might be expected, he was going to put the dog to work finding the girls. Mrs Hadaway, tearful and red-eyed through lack of sleep and worry, was standing at the police post with a man named Jack Twyman when Bishop came up. Thirty-year-old Twyman was employed by Keith Quick as a maintenance engineer on the Palace Pier, a job he had held for eleven years. He owned a dark blue Renault 16. He takes up the story: 'I drove to the Wild Park at 2 p.m. on 10 October. I drove into the park up past the pavilion, then turned and drove back. It was near there, in fact, by a seat at the foot of the steps referred to as Jacob's Ladder, that I saw Douggie Judd. He was standing in the middle of the track and I had to stop.'

Douglas Judd explained to him about the missing girls and introduced Twyman to Michelle Hadaway and Russell Bishop. 'Michelle, Russell and the dog, together with Judd, got into my car and drove to the police box in Lewes Road near the arch. This would now be around 2.30 p.m. Douggie got out of the car and went into the police box. He returned to the car within five minutes and said, "I nearly got arrested, they were so unhelpful, they don't want to know." We drove on to the Ditchling Road, where we stopped.'

Michelle and Jack walked into a field, calling the girls' names, while Bishop and Judd walked off down Ditchling Road in the direction of Ditchling Beacon. After a search made in the car to various other locations, including Stanmer Park and Forty-Nine Acres, Bishop got out with the dog and Judd, saying that they would walk across the golf course, then down the ski-slope back into the Wild Park. Michelle and Jack Twyman drove back to the cricket pavilion area where the car could be turned round. Michelle got out and sat on the grass. Minutes later, at 4.21 p.m., she saw a number of police officers running towards the wooded area behind the public toilets, towards a youth standing on a steep bank, waving a police constable's helmet. The distraught mother clambered back into the car, which Twyman moved towards a gathering crowd of excited individuals. The helicopter hovered overhead. A man with an Alsatian dog flagged the car down. He spoke to the terrified Michelle and saw tears pouring down her flushed cheeks. 'I wouldn't go any further my love, they've found the bodies.' Michelle Hadaway collapsed, sobbing.

Two lads had found the girls lying in an overgrown children's den.

Matthew Marchant, aged eighteen, unemployed, and Kevin Rowland, a hospital porter at Bevendean Hospital, aged nineteen, had been out searching since 3.30 p.m. They had decided to struggle through the undergrowth, trees and bushes that form the north-east perimeter of the Wild Park. Just after 4.20 p.m. they came to a stop on a steep, narrow, winding track leading up from the park to a row of houses at Coldean. They had found what appeared to be a large den, built of brambles and undergrowth. As they peered up the track, which turned to the left,

Marchant spotted something. He moved closer with some trepidation, but nothing could have prepared him for what came next. His eyes took in the colour of shocking pink. He edged closer, stooping down about fifteen feet away, then screamed out, 'Go and get the police, get someone!' Rowland took a brief look, then ran down the track, calling for help. White-faced, he burst from the copse like a rocket fired from its launcher. Waving frantically, he spotted Acting Police Sergeant Paul Francis (Smudger) Smith, walking across the park with Russell Bishop, Douggie Judd and Misty.

This officer's later statement to the Magistrate's Court provides a disturbing account of that afternoon.

'. . . On the tenth of October 1986 I was engaged in Barcombe Road, Moulsecoomb regarding two young girls who had been reported missing. At 4.05 p.m. I crossed the Lewes Road and entered the Wild Park. When I crossed the road I had a civilian with me, Miss Stevenson. I made my way into the Wild Park. At one stage I stopped to light my pipe. At this stage two men came up to me. Personally, I did not know them at that stage by name. I now know who one of them was. The man with the dog and stick was Russell Bishop. I don't know the name of the other [Douglas Judd].

'. . . I was about twenty to thirty yards from the entrance to the Park; that's when it goes on to the grass. I had a conversation with Russell Bishop. After the girls were found I went to the police station. That was the first opportunity I had to make up my pocket-book. I have made a note in my pocket-book of the conversation with Russell Bishop. I refer to him as the dog man.

'He said, "Have you been searching long?"

'I replied, "I have been searching here since eight o'clock this morning, what about you?"

'He said, "Me too. I came down early and even gave a statement."

'At that stage the other man, who hadn't said much, walked off. Russell Bishop said to me, "Do you think the kids are around here?"

'I replied, "I don't know, we haven't found them yet."

'Bishop then said, "I reckon they have gone north or, if they are here, they're finished."

'I said, "Well, Brighton has some strange people in it."

'Bishop said, "Yeah, I'm not searching any more."

'I then said, "Why not? You have a dog and it's still light."

'He then said to me, "No. I mean the Old Bill wouldn't believe it, would they?"

'I said, "What do you mean?"

'Bishop replied, "Well, if I found the girls and if they were done in, I would get the blame. I'd get nicked."

'We walked southwards away from the road into the park where it is grassed. A young lad came over the bank towards us. He was shouting, "We found them, somebody has found them." We then followed the youth and ran towards the pavilion by the bank.

'At this stage I am dressed in a Gannex coat and boots and I am not an athlete, so I said to Bishop, "You are faster than me. Find the boys who have found them and keep them and yourself away from the girls." When I said that he was running in front of me. I am sure he was in hearing range. He [Bishop] ran on ahead. After a short distance he disappeared from view into the undergrowth. I ran after him and went in roughly at the same spot. There was a woman with a child in a pushchair on the tree-line. I shouted through the undergrowth to where they were, as I couldn't see them. There were several replies. I crashed through the undergrowth and eventually came to a path.

MOULSECOOMB

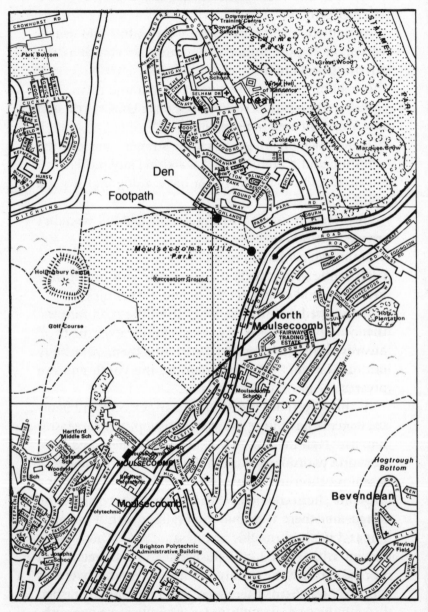

'When I came across the path it was leading upwards. The valley is not steep but you need to grab on to the undergrowth and trees to scramble up. It is walkable. As you are going up the path it turns to the left and that's where they were. I saw a lad in a grey jacket and from there to the girls was not a great distance . . .

'From the position I was in, crouched down [he is six foot six], you could see the outline of something particular. A shocking pink jumper or pullover. At that stage all you could really make out was the pink. There was something there not part of the vegetation. I went forward. The main thing I wanted to do was keep the youths away from what I presumed were the bodies. As I moved forward I could see the figure of a head and an arm thrown across. It was at this point I noticed that the chap in the grey jacket had a knife in his hand which I took to be a kitchen knife.

'I radioed up to the Moulsecoomb police box. I gave them my own call-sign which is Charlie Oscar 38. They answered. I gave them words to the effect of: I have found one of the girls dead and would like a senior officer present.'

A tape recording of his call gives this short dramatic message: 'I have found one of the girls, thanks to some local lads. She looks dead. I am not going to touch her. We are north of the pavilion, up the hill. It is very steep. I want a senior officer here now, please.'

Smith then crawled through the undergrowth and noted that there were two bodies. The girl in pink was lying on her back, as if asleep. He noticed she had froth on her mouth, a bruise on her lower jaw and what looked like dried blood on her nostrils. His shocked reactions are clearly conveyed as he carried on with his account.

'. . . It was my first murder. I was shocked when I saw

the bodies and I don't know if I became a bit emotional. I don't think so. I felt upset that we had found them dead. I might have profaned. I might have sworn. My usual term is "bastards". I was worried about the man in grey, he looked like death warmed up. I probably did. They all looked pretty shocked, including Bishop . . . They were all very quiet.'

At 4.25 p.m. a radio message was sent from the Wild Park to John Street police station, saying that the two girls had been found dead. Superintendent Tomlinson ordered a radio blackout immediately and was driven at high speed to the scene. A woman led him, scrambling and crawling, up the steep bank to be met by PCAS Smith. Moments later the two men were joined by Detective Superintendent Bernie Wells, Tomlinson's plainclothes counterpart.

The Babes in the Wood had been found. Now the complicated procedure of a murder hunt began and other actors would enter the stage to play out their grim roles.

4. A 'Major Incident'

The Sussex Constabulary, like every other police force in the United Kingdom, employs its own branch of highly trained personnel called 'Scenes of Crime' officers. This elite group is part and parcel of the CID, although not necessarily everyone in it is a serving police officer. They may be called to assist with any form of police investigation, including burglary, robbery and, of course, rape and murder.

Superintendent Tomlinson had requested the presence at the scene in the Wild Park of CID officers, his scenes of crime and photographic personnel, and a local pathologist. He gathered together Bishop, Marchant, Rowland and a woman witness who had been walking her dog in the park, and handed them over to Detective Constable Moreton, who was to take down their statements in his pocket-book. Tomlinson then directed that the area was to be sealed off with striped plastic tape.

Edward William Redman was the official scenes of crime investigator called to the park. Together with his team of experts – notably Stephen Fenner, Mark Baynes (photographer) and Geoffrey Taylor, a CID officer experienced in preparing plans – he drove there in a specially equipped vehicle containing the paraphernalia of their trade: red plastic tape, floodlights, protective suits, plastic sheeting, spades and the 'murder bag'.

An earlier notorious Sussex murder was responsible for the introduction of the latter item – the killing and burning of unfortunate Emily Kaye at the 'Officer's House' at the Crumbles, Eastbourne, in 1924. Patrick Mahon had clubbed Miss Kaye to death in his tiny cottage overlooking the steep white cliffs and the English Channel. When Home Office pathologist Bernard Spilsbury had arrived there, he found to his horror that Detective Chief Inspector Savage was using his bare hands to collect up pieces of decomposing flesh. 'Are there no rubber gloves?' Spilsbury asked with incredulity, concerned about the obvious risk of infection. Apparently not. Months later Scotland Yard, in consultation with Spilsbury and other eminent forensic scientists, devised and assembled a 'murder bag' that was to be taken to the scene of any violent crime in the future. Its contents include plastic exhibit bags, seals and labels; a knife and a small fork; tweezers and gloves; a magnifying glass and a tape measure.

The scenes of crime unit arrived just before 4.45 p.m., only minutes after receiving Tomlinson's message. Russell Bishop had been feeling sick and had vomited on the grass. He asked DC Moreton if he could get a lift home and Moreton waved over an unmarked Rover police car, traffic control vehicle Tango 670 manned by PC James Taylor. Bishop and his dog Misty were taken to Bishop's flat in Hollingdean and Tango 670 returned to the Wild Park to await further orders. Douglas Judd had left the park too, saying that he had a date that evening.

The 'Major Incident' van, parked outside the police box in Lewes Road, was moved under the direction of Inspector Chris Verrion to a 'forward position' in the Wild Park. Dozens of other police vehicles swarmed into the area and the press arrived *en masse* in private cars.

Lee Hadaway learned of his daughter's death over his car radio in a news bulletin. Barrie Fellows had been pacing to and fro outside Lewes Road police box with two of his brothers, Nigel and Kevin. At first he heard that the girls had been found at the pavilion, which he assumed to be the famous pavilion in the centre of Brighton. They were alive and well, cold and hungry. He was overcome with emotion. 'I'll give her a bloody good smack,' he said, holding back the tears. 'No, you won't, you'll give her a great big hug,' whispered Kevin, taking his brother by the arm. Minutes later a call came through to say that the girls had indeed been found, dead . . .

Fellows stood white-faced and stock-still. He began to tremble, then went berserk. Taking a swing at a constable, he was pinioned and thrown to the floor by his brothers. Forcibly held down, he sobbed and screamed, 'The fuckin' bastards, the fuckin' bastards.' Anxious for that exclusive picture, a press photographer, with the usual total disregard for private grief and a watchful eye on a fat cheque, climbed up to take a picture through the police box window. The shutter opened and closed. Nigel rushed out, saying that his brother had suffered an epileptic fit.

Television crews turned up with outside broadcasting units; parked discreetly in a side street was a white ambulance marked with a red cross. The driver and his assistants wore no uniform but were soberly dressed in dark grey suits and black shoes. The undertakers had arrived, albeit several hours too early.

Redman and his team, dressed in white polypropylene disposable suits, climbed the steep path to where the children lay. There they met an ashen-faced Smith, anxious to get home after his horrific experience. Before anything could be touched or moved, Baynes moved in with his camera. After carefully adjusting his lens and viewfinder and standing in the position from where Marchant and Rowland had caught their first glimpse of the bodies, he could just see something pink-coloured through the eyepiece of his Canon. He took nineteen photographs of the girls and the immediate surroundings. Each shot had to be taken with the precision of a wedding day photograph; he wouldn't get another chance. Later he put together Exhibit MLB/1, one of the most horrific photo albums in the history of recent crime.

Once Baynes had completed this task, Redman moved in and absorbed the scene before him. He made a few notes on a pad, then began to collect various items of potential evidence. Anything that by itself or together with other items might be useful in connecting the offence with a suspect, should one be apprehended, was carefully picked up and placed in its own clear plastic envelope, each labelled with Redman's initials and number. He collected 129 such items in all, beginning with EWR/1, a yellow-handled knife.

At the University of Lyon in France in 1910 Edmund Locard had formulated his 'exchange principle', in which he claimed that a criminal 'always without exception' leaves something behind at the scene of his crime which was not there before and, similarly, carries away something which was not on him when he arrived. This principle works in non-violent crimes as well. For example: a house-breaker who cuts himself in the process of climbing through a window he has just smashed may leave behind stains of his own blood on the window sill as vital evidence of his visit. He may also carry away with him fragments of glass and paint from the point of entry, which have lodged in his clothes.

Locard's principle is an important one. It is the embodiment of much of the thinking and practice upon which modern forensic science laboratories all over the world operate.

If we regard a crime as a complex event in history – for this is what it is, an interaction in time and space between people and things – it can be seen that each crime creates a unique set of problems. These problems do, nevertheless, have common themes and pose some basic, general questions applicable to all crimes. It is within the framework of such questions that the forensic scientist begins his work, providing information in the first instance to the investigating officer.

No doubt Redman bore in mind his training based upon these precepts as he went about collecting fibres at the crime scene in the woods. Using tweezers, he carefully removed them from the overhanging vegetation, labelling them EWR/2 to EWR/8. From near Nicola's fingertips he picked up Karen's knickers (EWR/9) and also the child's green school sweatshirt (EWR/10).

Deputy Police Surgeon Dr Christopher David Isaac arrived at 5.30 p.m. He examined the girls from a distance of five feet – in order not to disturb the scene, he was allowed no closer. He noted injuries to the face and neck areas, then certified both girls dead at the scene.

At 6.30 p.m. Dr Iain Eric West, Consultant Forensic Pathologist and head of the Department of Forensic Medicine at the United Medical Schools of Guy's and St Thomas' Hospitals, arrived at the scene. He examined the girls *in situ* under the watchful eye of Redman.

West recorded that Nicola Fellows was lying on her back at the opening to the cave-like clearing, near an elder tree, her left arm by her side, her right arm flexed across her chest. She appeared fully clothed. By her left hand lay articles of clothing, including what seemed to be Karen's knickers (which Redman, along with Karen's sweatshirt, had replaced for West's examination). Karen Hadaway lay face down and at right angles to Nicola, towards the farther end of the cave. Her right arm was extended over Nicola's body, her head resting over her own right arm and on Nicola's abdomen. She was not wearing knickers, but otherwise appeared fully clothed. Perhaps West had not noticed Karen's sweatshirt when he made that observation. Karen's grey pleated skirt was rucked up and her pink trainers were soiled with dirt. There were visible bruises round both girls' necks. West recorded a vivid crimson mark on Karen's throat, together with other marks covering her face. There was blood-flecked foam drying on Nicola's lips and her eyes were semi-closed in death.

Under West's direction, Redman wrapped the children's corpses in body-sheets before their removal at 7.53 p.m. to the Brighton Borough Mortuary. The undertakers carried out their task efficiently and without fuss. Although hardened to their work, they lifted their burdens with great respect, for they had young children themselves.

Dr West was acknowledged to be an expert in his field and the police expected him, if he could, to arrive at a conclusion as to how and when the girls met their untimely deaths. He knew the girls had been found at 4.21 p.m. and had been informed that both children had last been seen alive at around 6.45 p.m. the previous evening. His first and most important job was to attempt to ascertain the time of death.

This is done in part by taking the body temperature and, if possible, the temperature of the body's surroundings. Where bodies are found in the open, a probe can be inserted into the ground to check the ground temperature.

Under average conditions, a clothed body will cool in the air at the rate of two and a half degrees per hour for the first twelve hours. The body will lose heat more slowly as the temperature comes nearer to that of its surroundings. It should feel cold after about twelve hours, and the temperature of the internal organs should be the same as the environmental temperature in eighteen to twenty-four hours. Any internal thermometer reading will suffice, the most accurate coming from the rectum; the vagina should be avoided in order not to compromise any trace evidence resulting from sexual interference. Factors which slow the rate of cooling are a warm atmosphere, clothing and bedding, obesity and lack of ventilation. In this case, the bodies must have cooled at an optimum rate, for with the exception of clothing none of the other conditions was present.

There is, of course, a time limit beyond which body temperature ceases to be of value. It is normally agreed by forensic specialists that a reading should be taken if a person was known to be alive within eighteen hours of discovery. It is fair to say, though, that not all forensic pathologists subscribe to this view. The significance of information about time of death is that it may eliminate a suspect from further enquiry or help to consolidate suspicion in a particular direction. Post-mortem examination of a body's alimentary system might also establish the cessation of digestion, and thereby help to narrow down the time of death even further.

Dr West took neither of the vital temperature readings, later claiming that although he should have done so, he didn't because the bodies had been out in the open for nearly 24 hours, they were very cold to the touch and also he had left his ground probe in his car. Perhaps he had forgotten the other probe he always carried in his bag. He appears not to have considered the possibility that although the girls had been missing for nearly 24 hours, they could still have been murdered just some twelve hours before his examination, during the night or early morning; they would still then be cold to the touch.

As there were indications of sexual assault, West rightly decided not to take temperature readings from the anus or vagina of either child. However, there were two alternative methods he could have applied. One was to make a stab into the liver, although this would have the obvious disadvantage of disturbing and bloodying their clothing. The second option open to him would have been to insert a thermometer into the brain via the nose. It is accepted that brain temperature is not as reliable as core body temperature for estimating time of death, and the majority of pathologists in Britain would not use this method. All in all, the issue is a difficult one, involving a debate over professional judgement, but it should be said that in general a pathologist would be wise to take body temperatures if there is the slightest suspicion that time of death might become an issue. This suspicion should have been to the fore in the case of the Babes in the Wood and certainly the failure to take internal body temperature readings later became a controversial issue in the trial of Russell Bishop.

Dr West conducted his post-mortem examination on the two children at 8.30 p.m. on 10 October. Present were Detective Chief Superintendent John McConnell, the officer now in overall charge of the case; Superintendent Wells; Detective Inspector Bentham; Detective Sergeant Taylor (scenes of crime unit); Edward Redman; Mark Baynes; Mr A. Carpenter (closed circuit television); PCAS 835 Worth (HM Coroner's Office); Mrs F. Smith (HM Coroner's Office); and, finally, Dr Isaac, the police surgeon.

West concluded that the cause of death in both girls was compression of the neck consistent with manual strangulation. Karen had been sexually assaulted before she died; Nicola had been sexually assaulted twice, before and after death. The blood-flecked foam on Nicola's lips was a well-established characteristic of death by drowning or strangulation. He noted that hypostasis, or post-mortem lividity, had set in. This condition is described as the gravitational settling of blood within the blood vessels and does not occur until at least an hour or two hours after death. Its onset could be somewhat delayed if a body were moved soon after death. By pushing his thumbs into the flesh where lividity was present – where there was no whitening of the depressed area – Dr West deduced that the girls had indeed been dead for more than twelve hours.

He estimated that the girls had died between 5 p.m. on the 9th and around 3 a.m. and 4 a.m. on the 10th, later narrowing this down to between 7 p.m. and 8 p.m. on Thursday the 9th. He said it was a very tentative suggestion at the very best; he simply could not be sure.

This tragic day produced two immediate results. The first came in the early hours of Saturday morning. At 2.30 a.m. Russell Bishop and Jennie Johnson were woken by police officers hammering on their front door. DC Paul Gibson and WPC Corkill were standing on the step when Jennie opened it to them. Bishop was in bed when the officers entered the house; beside him lay a young child asleep. The police had ascertained that Bishop had been seen in the Wild Park shortly before the girls had disappeared and that he had been in the very same area when they were found dead. Having already checked his name on the National Police Computer, they knew that Bishop had 'form' for theft and drug abuse; he was also known to the Drugs Squad as an informer. This combination of facts led the case officers to view him with some suspicion and they now made an appointment to interview him again later that day.

The second and perhaps more vital break in the investigation came with the re-discovery of the 'Pinto' sweatshirt, which Yann Svenski had left draped on a railing near Moulsecoomb railway station.

Robert Gander, a chartered engineer who lived in Hove and worked for the South Eastern Electricity Board, had been visiting a 132 kV electricity sub-station near Moulsecoomb railway station at 3.30 p.m. on Friday afternoon. A short road runs off Woodside School Road up to the sub-station, alongside a footpath from Woodside School Road to the northern end of Crespin Way. He parked his brown Austin Montego saloon outside the sub-station gates and began to unload a few plans and drawings from the boot. He noticed a woman looking at a garment on the footpath and saw her give it a toss with her foot. It looked to Gander to be some sort of jumper and, mindful of the hunt for the missing children, he picked it up; it was the sweatshirt discovered by Svenski in the small hours of that morning. It stank of body odour and there was also some red staining on the chest area and right cuff.

Gander telephoned the police, asked if he could drop off the garment at Lewes Road police box and at 4.10 p.m. he handed it over to PC David Edwards at the 'incident post', a Portakabin temporarily moved alongside the police box. Edwards made a note of Gander's name and address, then placed the sweatshirt in a brown paper bag which he stowed on a shelf; its label, a yellow message form (G19), showed Gander's initials (REG/1). The label itself was also allocated an identification number, DE/2, to signify that it was PC Edwards's second exhibit of the day. Inspector Chris Verrion took the garment with him on his return to John Street police station and placed it in the 'Exhibit Store' next to the 'Major Incident Room'. He didn't realise it, but Gander had given the police the killer's sweatshirt.

5. Statements

Distraught parents Michelle and Lee Hadaway sobbed as they spoke of their daughter's death and of the killer they were convinced Karen knew. According to her mother, 'It was definitely someone she knew or they both knew. I would be very surprised if it was a stranger.' She went on, 'Even if it was a stranger who spoke to her, Karen would have run. She was that sort of girl.' Although not proof of evidence that could indicate who the killer might be, this statement cannot be ignored. It could indeed be the first rung on a ladder that might well in time tell us who that killer is: it is, after all, the case that in over half the murders committed the victim and the murderer know each other, through a family relationship or by close acquaintance.

Michelle looked close to collapse as she described the effect of the killings on her other two children. 'Lyndsey has been told the truth and she cried but I don't think she really understands. She is just missing Karen at the moment. Darren, who is at a boarding school for slow learners, came home at the weekend but asked to go back because it was all too upsetting.' Tearfully, she said that Karen had been given all the usual warnings about strangers: 'You do your best, you can't keep the children locked up, you have to give them freedom. It's just the society we live in.' Clutching a tear-stained handkerchief, she finished: 'I knew my daughter and she knew our standards. Perhaps I was over-protective, but she knew she wasn't to talk to strangers and we'd like to think she never did.'

While a serious case such as this brings to the fore hundreds of individuals anxious to assist the police, there are inevitably the time wasters and the sensation-seekers who for spurious reasons of their own concoct a story to attract attention.

Tracey Anne Cox was born on 24 April 1970 and, unemployed, lived with her parents at 65 Newick Road. She was a friend of Marion Stevenson and Russell Bishop and had accompanied them on the call at the Fellows' home during the afternoon of 9 October, when Bishop had enquired after Douglas Judd.

Tracey Cox remembered Nicola's shout through the letterbox, though she chose to embellish the remark as, 'See you – fucking old slag!' Marion Stevenson stated to the police that she had been patiently waiting for Russell Bishop to turn up for the date he had promised her. At a few minutes after 6 p.m., Tracey Cox had joined Stevenson at her garden gate, waited with her until 6.30 p.m., then left and returned to her own home, intending to go to the fish and chip shop in Coldean Lane. Her route would take her into Newick Road, left into Barcombe Road, across Lewes Road and up into Coldean Lane. However, Cox stated that she had left Stevenson at about 6.10 p.m. and estimated that she arrived at the fish and chip shop at 6.20 p.m.

It was there, she claimed in her first statement, that she saw Nicola and Karen standing on the forecourt, playing conkers together: 'I was in the shop about five minutes and when I came out Nicola and Karen were still there.

They spoke to me, asking if I could get them some conkers from the trees opposite at the entrance to Stanmer Park. I told them I couldn't go across and Karen asked me where I was going. In fact it was Nicky who asked me to get conkers and Karen who asked me where I was going. I recall that Karen was wearing a Coldean School top, which was either grey or green, crew-necked with a Coldean School motif. I cannot recall what Nicky was wearing.'

On the face of it, this account seemed to correspond with that of Mrs Green and Alan Vickery. Then Cox elaborated on her sighting and discussion with the girls, claiming that she last saw them about 6.45 p.m. as she walked into the railway tunnel en route to a friend's house in Birdham Road. But another witness came forward who placed Tracey Cox in another location at roughly the same time. Cox was re-interviewed several times, and each interview revealed more inaccuracies. In her final statement she admitted: 'Where I have stated in my previous statements that I went to the fish and chip shop in Coldean Lane and saw the girls playing outside, I now realise I was mistaken when I made those statements. I did not go to the fish and chip shop in Coldean Lane on the evening of Thursday, 9th October 1986; however, to the best of my recollection, I did go there on the previous evening. At no time did I see Nicola and Karen playing conkers on Thursday evening, 9 October. However, I think I may have seen them playing conkers on a previous occasion. I do not recall seeing Nicola and Karen on Wednesday, 8 October either.'

Tracey Cox was given the opportunity on two occasions to contribute to this book. One letter was returned torn in half, the second ignored.

Witnesses were coming forward in their droves, sometimes more of a hindrance than a help. A customer at the

Hiker's Rest pub, having consumed ten pints of lager, decided to conduct his own search for the missing girls during the evening of 9 October. Without a torch, he stumbled around the Wild Park, hammering on car windows and generally making a nuisance of himself. On banging on one courting couple's car he was told to 'piss off', or words to that effect. It is a wonder he could have found the Wild Park at all after downing that quantity of drink, let alone reconnoitre the area without being spotted by dozens of other searchers. Despite his paralytic state, however, it seems he could recall times to the minute, could detail what he was wearing and where he fell to the finest degree of accuracy.

One young girl claimed that when Karen went to the local shop on 9 October she was being followed by a friend of the Hadaway family, a person also known to the Fellowses. This man, who can only be referred to anonymously as Mr A, should have been some five miles away at that time and indeed claimed to the police that he was.

The police were interviewing all known sex offenders at length, with one notable exception. But with a growing list of child molesters waiting to be interviewed at Brighton, they persisted in efforts to accumulate evidence against a man who in the past had committed no graver offence than stealing from a motor vehicle.

It now seemed that Russell Bishop was one of the last people to see the girls alive. Roy Dadswell, the Park Constable, had had a brief conversation with Bishop before he finished his duty at 6.30 p.m. on 9 October. Bishop had strolled up to Dadswell, and called out, 'I haven't seen you for a while.' Dadswell replied, 'Oh, I've been around.' Bishop went on to explain that his car had broken down in Coldean Lane and Dadswell remarked, 'You'll probably have to get it repaired,' to which Bishop replied, 'Oh, I'll repair it myself.' A short conversation followed, which involved football. Bishop then showed Dadswell a scar on his left shoulder. They said goodbye and parted company. Dadswell timed this chat at about 5.15 p.m., with the meeting lasting five to six minutes. Bishop later recalled to the police that he had seen Nicola and Karen swinging on a tree in the Wild Park; this was also confirmed by Dadswell, who had told the girls to be careful and to get down. Later, at about 6.15 p.m., Bishop was seen walking along Lewes Road by two men on their way home from work, having already apparently been spotted in Lewes Road from a passing bus, at about 6 p.m., by his uncle, Ted Dawes. Bishop, as we know, was supposed to meet Marion Stevenson outside her Barcombe Road home at about 6.30 p.m. He didn't turn up.

As Saturday, 11 October drew to a close, Bishop was interviewed for a second time, this time by Detectives Barry Evans and Doug Penry. The details Bishop had supplied earlier did not fit with the puzzle. He had claimed that he had seen the two bodies and described how the girls were huddled together: Nicky lying on her back with Karen's head resting on her stomach. He had stated that he went over to them, felt the pulse of each girl in turn and noticed that they were cold and stiff, that they were obviously dead. He described the blood-flecked foam on Nicola's lips.

The interviewing officers now knew for a fact that Bishop had not been within twelve yards of the bodies, that the girls were surrounded by undergrowth and therefore that he could not have noticed these details. PC Smith had already stated that he had not mentioned any of these facts to Bishop when he returned from checking the bodies, so how could Bishop have known the gruesome details? The police took away all the clothing Bishop claimed he had worn on 9 October, including a pair of Lois jeans, a blue jumper, a pair of white underpants and a pair of black slip-on shoes. Later that night, Bishop was traced to the Hiker's Rest pub in Coldean Lane and driven to John Street police station to be questioned further about his earlier statements.

The interviewing officers went out of their way to explain the severity of the situation Bishop was placing himself in. He now claimed that he had imagined it all, made it up to make himself look important. He had not gone into the den: 'I was mistaken. I intended to do this [check the pulses, etc] but did not.' Changing his account yet again, he said: 'I am confused. I did check their pulses.'

Not only PC Smith but also Marchant and Rowland, the young men who had found the bodies, denied that Bishop had been near the girls. Russell Bishop was rapidly drowning in a sea of deceit. Eventually he said that he hadn't touched the children. He became agitated and refused to speak another word.

It was certainly true that Bishop's red Ford Escort had 'blown up'. He had left it, parked half on the pavement, at the top end of Coldean Lane at the junction of Ditchling Road where it was spotted by local residents, among them a retired gentleman called Buckwell who lived in the Bromley Road area of Brighton. At about 3 p.m. on 9 October Buckwell had left his home to walk to the post office in Ditchling Road to collect his pension. He noticed the Escort parked halfway on to the pavement outside a public building just above the viaduct and the Upper Ditchling Road. The vehicle, he noted, was still there the following day.

In his initial interviews with the police, Bishop had claimed that after leaving Dadswell he had crossed the busy Lewes Road to buy an *Evening Argus* newspaper: 'The shop may remember me as I found that I had no money to pay for the newspaper and had to come away without one . . . I then walked home.' The shop assistant did indeed know Russell Bishop but said, 'He never came into my shop that afternoon.' Bishop had then said that he walked diagonally back across Lewes Road towards the Wild Park and Brighton, but turned right by Moulsecoomb Library up to Moulsecoomb railway station and back into the Hollingdean Estate, into Stephen's Road and home.

Bishop's statement that he had no money when he entered the newsagents was a lie. According to his third statement, dated 15 October, he had had some £5 on him: 'I picked up the *Evening Argus* newspaper from a bundle of others and briefly looked at the front page, although I do not recall what was on that page. I went to get the £5 note from my pocket but found it to be missing. I assumed I must have lost it. There were other people being served at this time and it is possible that no one saw me do this.'

This account of his visit to the newsagent's shop not only contradicted his story of being embarrassed at the counter but is contradicted itself by his next statement that he then purchased some drugs from a friend called Angie, smoking his joint in the public toilet next to the police box in Lewes Road. His story concludes with the claim that he was back home by 6 p.m., thus displaying a remarkable ability to be in two places at the same time, for he had earlier claimed to the police that his uncle, Ted Dawes, had seen him from a bus in Lewes Road at 6 p.m. In addition to that, other witnesses who knew him well, his friend Kevin Doyle among them, saw Bishop emerging from the Wild Park just above the point where the railway crosses Lewes Road at around 6.30 p.m. None of them noticed what he was wearing but, tying this in with Ted Dawes' alleged sighting, Bishop was certainly not home at 6 p.m., thereby tending to confirm his own account that he smoked a joint in the public toilet near the police box and just a few yards from the railway arch.

Despite Dr West's amended conclusion that about 7 p.m. was the earliest time of death of the two girls, the police persisted in the notion that they had been murdered between 5.15 p.m. and 6.30 p.m. I believe they acted on this supposed time of death in order to fit in with Bishop's alleged movements.

The police later went to some lengths to check out Ted Dawes' alleged sighting; Dawes himself had gone to America. David O'Neil, a bus driver for the past twenty years who worked for the Brighton & Hove Bus and Coach Company, was asked by the police some four weeks after the murders if he recalled seeing a man, aged about 50, wearing a grey suit and Dr Scholl sandals, travelling on his bus during the afternoon of 9 October. This was a tall order by any stretch of the imagination – with thousands of people using his bus in the course of a month, it is not surprising that O'Neil could 'not be sure', although he did have a 'slight recollection'. What O'Neil could tell the police about his duty that day was that he changed shift with driver R. Baker at 5.25 p.m. at the south-west corner of the Old Steyne in Brighton's town centre. George Baker, a bus inspector and no relative of the second driver, was later asked to confirm this change-over of drivers, which he did. The police also learned that the first ticket issued after this change in shifts was at 5.41 p.m.

Detective Constable Brian Lee, an experienced officer who might have been better employed on more pressing

enquiries, was allocated the task of checking the route, a
job a traffic constable might have accomplished with ease
and rather less waste of public money. Drowning in
complacency, the Sussex Constabulary, with its abysmal
crime detection rate and its extremely high profile with
traffic duties, seemed to have its priorities wrong. D C Lee
clambered aboard a number 25 bus which had stopped at
the Pavilion Parade, the earliest connecting bus that
would have taken Dawes to Coldean Lane. Lee noted in
his pocket-book that on this trip it was raining and that his
bus was crawling as it arrived at the Vouge gyratory
system at 6 p.m., reaching the police box in Lewes Road,
the spot where Bishop claimed Uncle Ted saw him, just
after 6 p.m. More police manpower and expense was
deployed when WPC Clarke, travelling in an unmarked
police vehicle, picked up a rather bored DC Lee and conveyed him back to John Street, where he could finish his
shift with a cup of tea. Perhaps the police would have been
more usefully employed checking on other witnesses who
did have vital evidence but who were never approached
by them until this book was researched.

The police had already removed from Bishop's house
the clothes he said he was wearing on the 9th. It was
several days later that the significance of the 'Pinto'
sweatshirt began to be realised, discovered as it had been
on the night of 9/10 October on the very same route
Bishop said he walked home, a mere yard or two from his
path.

In an attempt to pin down Bishop's movements that
day, the police talked to the two people most closely
involved with him: his common-law wife, Jennie
Johnson, and his girlfriend, Marion Stevenson.

Jennifer Nancy Johnson was born on 4 November
1965. She is a pert little blonde, very attractive, with a slim

figure. Her first statement to the police was made on 18
October 1986:

'I live at 17 Stephen's Road, Brighton, with my
common-law husband, Russell Bishop, and our son of
twelve months, Victor. I am due to have a second child in
the December of this year. I live in Stephen's Road in the
ground-floor flat of a council block and have done so for
just over a year.' She went on: 'We moved in on 19
December 1985. Prior to this we lived in a bed and
breakfast accommodation at 24 Vernon Terrace,
Brighton. Prior to this we were in similar accommodation
at 12 George's Terrace, Brighton. We were at this address
for about three months. When I first lived with Russell,
we stayed at his parents' house at 46 Coldean Lane,
Brighton. I had known Russell for the past three years and
I have been living with him for two years. I knew Russell,'
she said, 'through CB radio and I was an enthusiast at this
time and living at home at 106 Harefield Avenue, Bevendean. Up until the beginning of this year, my relationship
with Russell was not happy. He had formed a relationship
with Marion Stevenson of Barcombe Road, Moulsecoomb. Due to this relationship, Russell left home and
moved in with Marion to bed and breakfast accommodation somewhere in Benton Terrace, Brighton. As far as I
can remember, he was only at this address for about a
month. Other than this occasion, I ignored the times
when he was out fishing and any other place he would
spend the night.

'I am able to confirm that on Thursday, 9 October 1986 I
left home at 8 a.m. to attend the Sussex County Hospital at
8.45 a.m. I took my son Victor with me. Russell was at
home when I left.'

She made the journey by bus, which invites the question: why didn't Bishop give her a lift? He claimed that he

went into Brighton at about 8.45 a.m. to go bait-digging on the beach opposite Holland Road, Hove, so he could have taken her to the hospital en route.

She continued, 'I returned home at about 12 noon. Russell was at home when I returned. From speaking to Russell I learned that the engine of his motor car had "gone" and that he had left the motor car in Ditchling Road, abandoned . . .'

Bishop had not gone bait-digging at all and his car broke down in the opposite direction to that of Hove.

'Russell and I watched the new detective programme which started about 1.35 p.m. and ended at about 2.30 p.m. Present at our address was also a friend, Tracey Bonsu. I remember that Russell and I had an argument about who was going to look after Victor, and Russell left about 2.45 p.m.'

Tracey Bonsu recalled that Bishop was wearing jeans and a dull, grey-coloured sweatshirt.

Johnson continued 'I was at home with Tracey until Tracey and I left at about 4 p.m. and I took Victor to a friend called Sonia. She was to look after Victor for me. I remember leaving my home at about 3.35 p.m. Russell was still out when I left home.'

Sonia Maskell recalled babysitting for her that day.

'On Thursday, 9 October this year, Jennie came to my flat with Victor, her son, and a friend of hers she introduced as Tracey. I do not know her surname. Jennie got here about 4 p.m. and left for work at about 4.45 p.m. She said that Russell hadn't returned home and she still didn't know where he was. Jennie got back from work to here about 7.40 p.m. and left my home about 9 p.m.'

Johnson worked as a cleaner at the American Express offices in Brighton. In her statement dated 13 October, taken down by Bishop's solicitor, Ralph Haeems, she significantly contradicts Sonia Maskell's timing. Sonia claimed that Johnson left her with her son Victor at about 9 p.m. that evening, but in her statement Johnson now claims, 'On Thursday, 9 October 1986, I left work at about 7.25 p.m., catching a bus at about 7.30 p.m., and went to Sonia's house to collect Victor. Sonia was not at home when I collected Victor and the only people present were Sonia's four children. Sonia telephoned her home when I was there and I spoke to her. I left Sonia's home at about 8.10 p.m. to 8.15 p.m. and walked to an off-licence, which took about two to three minutes. I walked home, arriving about 8.25 p.m. En route I bought some cigarettes and two packets of crisps. Russell was home. After a couple of minutes Russell asked me to go out to the off-licence. I left and bought two packets of crisps and some chocolate and returned home. I was away for about five minutes. I am able to recall Russell was at home in the armchair wearing a dressing gown. I understand that he had had a bath.'

The police were no doubt confused over the timings given by Jennie Johnson, but they were more unhappy when they took a statement from another cleaner employed by American Express. '. . . Jennie was saying that Russell had come in after 11 p.m. the night before [9 October] and had washed all of his clothes. She [Jennie] thought that was odd because she said he had only put them on clean that evening. She didn't say anything else about it that night but I do recall on another occasion after the girls had been found and Russell had been seen by the police, Jennie saying that Russell couldn't have done the killings because he had told her that he had been in the pub all evening.'

What is perhaps the most damaging aspect of this statement, if it is correct, is that Johnson makes the point that Bishop had changed into clean clothes that evening. By her own admission, she claims she did not see him between the time he left home at 2.45 p.m. until she arrived home either at 8.25 p.m. or just after 9 p.m., when he was wearing a dressing gown. So how did she know that he had changed his clothes that afternoon?

Marion Stevenson, at sixteen, had fallen in love with Bishop. Easily influenced by his boasts and lies, she became infatuated with him; caring not a jot for the fact that Bishop was living with Jennie Johnson, who was bearing his child, she saw him whenever she could. Unlimited sex was high on Bishop's list of priorities and he found a willing and insatiable partner in Stevenson, later admitting to me and the press that she was simply his 'bit on the side'. Maybe she believed his promises to marry her one day and have children.

Stevenson had been seduced at the tender age of eight years old by one Ernest Pullen who, according to his black and gold business card, specialises in photographs, stills and videos. He had served a prison sentence for engaging in sexual intercourse with a minor and was released two days after Marion's sixteenth birthday.

Bishop had promised to meet Stevenson at about 6.30 p.m. on 9 October, but did not turn up. So what was his excuse? Marion claimed that when she tackled Russell about standing her up, he told her he had not met her that evening because Jennie had had severe stomach pains and he had stayed at home to look after his son while Jennie went to hospital. Marion was no doubt disappointed when Bishop didn't arrive to take her out that evening. In high expectation, she had dressed herself in her favourite green dress and waited by her front gate. At 6.05 p.m. Tracey Cox had arrived and they chatted together. At 6.30 p.m. Tracey left Marion. It was now getting dark and the street lamps were switched on. Marion realised that

Russell had stood her up. Needing cigarettes, she went to her room, took £1.50 from her coat pocket and wandered up through the subway to the off-licence at the Hiker's Rest pub, where she bought twenty Benson and Hedges.

Questioned for eleven hours, she was asked repeatedly if she had been with Bishop on the evening of the killings. She kept saying, 'No, no.' Eventually she gave way and said, 'Yes.' That false admission could have landed her in serious trouble, but fortunately she had an alibi: she had been babysitting with a friend in Brighton.

One might believe that it says a great deal for Stevenson's love that she believes Bishop to be innocent to this very day. She was to say publicly in the *Evening Argus*, referring to Karen and Nicola: 'I loved them both, I was like a big sister to Karen. She was often round my house, turning to me any time she wanted advice. She was here the day before it happened. My world fell apart the day they were found. I wanted to help Karen through life, to make sure she didn't make the same mistake I did. Every time I think about them, I cry.'

In desperation, Marion called upon Ernest Pullen, on whom she could rely on for a continuous supply of drugs and drink. The 58-year-old Pullen was dressed in an RAF uniform, which he was not entitled to wear, while she cried on his shoulder. He seduced her into sex, with his ever-watchful video recording every detail. Evidence of this screening exists to turn even the most hardened person's stomach. Pullen has photographed Stevenson naked dozens of times. He openly enjoys a sickening desire to be near very young children and boasts of his desires.

At the police station, the officers tried a different tack. After accepting a cigarette, Bishop was asked about a Pullen video that Marion Stevenson had 'starred' in.

Bishop now claimed to the police that he was worried (as was Michelle Hadaway) that Marion might have taken the two girls to Pullen's flat.

Stevenson undoubtedly muddied the waters in an article that later appeared in the *News of the World*, alleging that she had seen a pornographic movie showing one of Barrie Fellows' friends having sex with Nicola. The paper printed a retraction, but not until it had published an article implying that Fellows had attempted to blackmail the paper, promising not to complain to the Press Council about the article in return for £4000. Fellows became the target of a hate campaign, neighbours remembering his previous promotion of pornographic videos. Graffiti were plastered over his council house home: 'Child Molester Out'. A hangman's noose was found on his garden gate. He has described through tears of rage and grief how gossips had tarnished his daughter's memory: that the girls had been part of a child porn ring, that they had regularly enjoyed sex romps in the park, that Nicola had starred in a Dutch porno movie, that she had often been beaten up by her father, that she had had sex with her father and his friends, that her father had convictions for molesting children. 'The lies about me are bad enough, but it really takes warped minds to suggest these little girls were corrupted.'

Ernest Pullen's home was raided by the Drugs Squad on Monday, 13 October 1986 and he was arrested for possessing a quantity of cannabis. The police searched through Pullen's video collection but did not confiscate a single tape or bother to check Pullen's alibi for the night of the killings. Russell Bishop had been released from custody in the early hours of 12 October.

The press had been busy nosing out suspected child molesters. A popular Sunday newspaper ran an article in which it was reported that the brother-in-law of television's *Childwatch* presenter, Esther Rantzen, had also been questioned by police investigating the deaths of the two Brighton schoolgirls in the 'Babes in the Wood' murder hunt but had subsequently been eliminated from any further enquiries. It emerged that 45-year-old Nigel Vincent, the brother of Desmond Wilcox, Esther's husband, who had changed his name by deed poll, had been quizzed while on probation in connection with a sex offence.

A further newspaper allegation involved Russell Bishop's acknowledgement that he had fondled girls. This apparently came out in the wake of the 'Babes in the Wood' murders when he was questioned about sex attacks on five schoolgirls. Top Mormon and Freemason Leslie Scarthe was also reported to have admitted similar allegations.

'The Mormon connection came to light when police quizzed 60-year-old Scarthe about Karen and Nicola found just a few hundred yards from his church. A fifteen-year-old girl, Sarah (not her real name), told in a sworn affidavit how Scarthe had fondled her after she was sent to stay with him during school holidays when she was ten years of age. The girl added, "I can remember at least two occasions when he kissed me on the lips and asked me if I loved him. I told him I didn't. Another time, he took me to a beach and told me to take my clothes off and go into the sea nude. He tried to kiss and put his arms around me. I told him if he didn't stop I'd tell.'

This exposure followed a letter from a member of the public directed to Ralph Haeems, Bishop's solicitor. Having obtained a copy of this correspondence, I made further enquiries. The original complaint about Scarthe's activities had been made by the child's parents to the

Bishop of Sussex. It was alleged in this correspondence that Bishop Price minimises the allegations and did not want to hear any more evidence of any things that had been done to other girls other than Sarah. Another girl and her mother went to see Bishop Price, who referred them to his superior, Anthony Paternoster. Paternoster interviewed all the complainants, mothers and children, and instructed that the parents were to say nothing more about the incidents.

The parents, obviously unhappy with Paternoster's stance, decided to take their complaint to the Church's own Social Services Department at Solihull, which encompassed Scarthe's Church of Jesus Christ of Latterday Saints. The head of this department was John McLaverty. One of the complainants telephoned him on Thursday, 27 November 1986 to be told it was clearly a matter for the police. McLaverty promised to phone back the following day. He didn't. The parents went to the police and also complained to the Sussex County Council Education Authority.

The majority of Freemasons would have no truck with this kind of sexual harassment of minors committed by one of their brothers. Nevertheless, I received an anonymous phone call during my investigation to the effect that should Freemasonry be mentioned in this book, the book would not be published. It has been mentioned, the book is published and Lesley Scarthe received a prison sentence for unlawful sex with minors.

After Bishop had been found innocent of all charges, yet another newspaper story carried the astonishing headline, 'Police used sixteen-year-old girl as sex bait'. The article related how sexy sixteen-year-old Marion Stevenson was asked by the police to sleep with Russell Bishop. The idea was that the police were seeking a bedroom confession to the 'Babes in the Wood' murders. Although Jennie Johnson was Bishop's steady girlfriend, Marion was nevertheless supposed to be his secret lover.

Marion, according to the newspaper report, revealed that a police sergeant told her to make love to Bishop, and to ask him if he had killed the two little girls. What she was not told by the police, so it was claimed, was that their bedroom would be bugged. Although shocked, Marion went along with the idea because she believed that Russell Bishop was innocent. However, when they were alone in their love nest, Russell found the bug, but she eventually managed to persuade him that it was the only one and that the police would not be listening.

Marion said that she and Russell made passionate love for a very long time and, guessing by then that the police must be listening through their bugging device, she laid on a bravura performance for their benefit, crying out in delight and ecstasy. Passion spent, they lay together on the bed and she nerved herself to ask Bishop if he knew anything about the murder of the 'Babes in the Wood'. Calling her by her affectionate pet name of 'Maz', he assured her that he could not possibly have done anything like that. Clinging to her as he wept like a child, Russell Bishop told her vehemently that whoever had done it should be hanged.

This bugging – if indeed it ever took place – would have happened at 17 Stephen's Road without consent from either Bishop or Jennie Johnson. The police would have acted without any lawful right and any evidence gained from such a bugging operation could not have been admitted as evidence. Yet while there is only Stevenson's word and a newspaper article to support the Stephen's Road bugging as having occurred at all, it is interesting to learn that another premises was bugged. Rosalind Stevenson,

Marion's mother, gave consent for a Home Office tape recording service to be installed by the police in her home in an authorised attempt to entrap Bishop. The instrument was attached to the telephone. Marion made good use of it; for several weeks, every word Bishop uttered on the telephone was recorded at the police station and written down. Marion even routed an unopened letter sent by Bishop to her directly to the police.

A distraught Susan Fellows was sitting on her daughter's bed. A bed Nicola would never sleep in again. She and her husband had been tearfully recalling Nicola's wish to get married one day. She had even had a boyfriend at school. His name was Alex. Susan's trembling fingers held a note, the last words ever written by Nicky: 'To Alex, do you . . .?' The parents would never know what Nicola intended to add to her message. Her concentration had been broken when she was called out to play.

Susan, searching the Wild Park for her missing daughter on 9 October, had heard a shout of 'Mum' at about 6.45 p.m. It is probable, therefore, that at the time Russell Bishop was seen walking along Lewes Road the two girls were still alive.

Barrie Fellows described the murderers as animals without conscience. Looking tired and unshaven, smoking heavily, he said he could not get out of his mind how his daughter must have struggled as she was strangled. 'Imagine a child watching as her friend is being killed, it's terrible. It never should have happened. You hear about these things from the newspapers but you never think it's going to happen to you.'

Back at Wild Park, the scene of crime was bathed in arc lights. Two constables stood shivering in the cold night air.

A few yards away a lonely tree swayed in the wind, the tree the girls had been seen swinging on by the Park Constable and by Russell Bishop. A card attached to the white-ribboned spray of flowers at its base read: 'Karen and Nicola, never forgotten. The families.'

6. Russell Bishop

At 10 a.m. on 11 October Stephen Fenner returned with Edward Redman to the Wild Park to continue their search for vital clues. The location was guarded by uniformed police officers. The two men crouched down under the red tape and made their way up the track to make a further detailed search. Redman removed items of soil and clothing fibres which he labelled EWR/11 to EWR/17. Fenner was also systematically collecting every article he could lay his experienced hands on from an area 80 yards either side of the children's den. His first find was a yellow-handled hairbrush (SJF/1), then a piece of blue ribbon, a grey jumper, a white shoe. He entered the den and gathered up three pornographic magazines (SJF/4, SJF/5 and SJF/6). Other items, ranging from lengths of wood to pieces of tinfoil, wire and rubber pipe were all bagged up and labelled. The collection seemed endless.

As the clock ticked round to 11 a.m., PC Barry Markham, on duty at Brighton police station, was ordered to take over the Exhibit Store of the Major Incident Room. He noticed that there was one item of clothing in a brown paper bag without a label. It was the blue 'Pinto' sweatshirt found by Robert Gander.

At 2.30 p.m. Dr Anthony Peabody, a senior staff member at the Home Office Forensic Science Laboratory, arrived at the park wearing a dark blue boiler suit. He began to search for clues with Redman, and labelled eleven items AJP/1 to AJP/11. Redman was still busy with his tweezers and collected twelve more items, including a piece of wood, more fibres, a jam jar which had become entangled in undergrowth at the base of a tree, and the second of two blue fibres. He labelled them EWR/18 to EWR/29.

During the afternoon of 15 October Redman carefully examined the 'Pinto' sweatshirt, now labelled DE/1, and discovered several stains and small holes. He carried out a 'Kastlemeyer Blood Test' on the garment and found a slightly positive reaction for blood. To enable this to be done, Detective Inspector Chris Bentham took the sweatshirt from its brown wrapping and supported it on a piece of card, before placing it inside a clear polythene bag; it had already been photographed by Baynes as an exhibit.

Six individuals had by now given statements to the effect that Bishop owned and wore this garment, though they were never called to give evidence and I respect their wishes not to be named in this book. Michael Evans, one of Bishop's car-repairing friends, had already identified one of Bishop's sweatshirts as being pale blue with a name written on the chest. Evans also claimed that Bishop had described the two girls' bodies to him: 'One was lying on her back with the other lying across the other's stomach. One had blood coming from the corner of her mouth.' Michelle Hadaway, on the other hand, recalls that on 9 October Bishop was wearing a pale-coloured sweatshirt with a white diagonal stripe across the chest. Still, faced with Bishop's lies and a general belief that the discarded 'Pinto' sweatshirt did belong to him – despite appeals, no other owner had come forward to claim it – the police decided to interview him again and on 31 October paid another visit to his home.

Stephen's Road in the Hollingdean Estate is just as solid three-iron shot from the Hollingbury gold course. The name Hollingbury derives from Hollingbury Camp, one of the great Iron Age forts of Sussex built about 250 BC. Though its grassy ramparts may now easily be climbed, they were originally faced by a wall of timbers with a deep ditch in front, unscaleable without ladders.

Alderman Sir Herbert Carden bought over 12,000 acres of downland; the northern slopes of Hollingbury Park, 90 acres in extent, became known as Moulsecoomb Wild Park. Between 1895 and 1936 Sir Herbert sold most of the land to Brighton Borough Council. The Corporation, with its expanding housing policy, decided that part of the area could well suit their housing requirements and during the early 1950s built a large council estate due south of the Wild Park. Carden's name was recorded for posterity with an avenue and a hill called after him. Stephen's Road is just one of dozens of streets, culs-de-sac and roads that now make up the Hollingdean Estate. Number 17 is a ground-floor single-bedroomed flat in a block of similar dwellings. The spacious, open-plan back garden gives a panoramic view across the valley to Ditchling Road. There are shops and schools close by, a regular bus service runs into Brighton and the Bishops were not short of neighbours of a similar age.

Life with Russell, as Jennie freely admitted, was not entirely a bed of roses, but she was very much in love with him and tolerated his wild, easy-come, easy-go ways as best she could. The police in the past had been frequent visitors to their home and it came as no surprise when, once again, they were hammering on the

front door. It was 8.20 a.m. Outside was a maroon police
Ford Escort: it was unmarked, but the whip aerial on the
boot revealed its identity. 'It's the bloody filth, Russ, what
have you fuckin' done now?' Peering through the partially open door, Bishop took in the figures of Detective
Sergeant Phil Swan and Detective Constable Dave
Wilkinson. The officers sat down, reminded Bishop that
he had made several previous statements to the police,
and said they now wanted to take him in for further
questioning.

In one of his earlier statements, Bishop had said he had
fallen in some dog excrement, which was why he had
washed his clothing on the night of the murders. They
now drove him in the unmarked car to an area of grass in
Woodside Road and began the unsavoury task of seeking
the dog's droppings. Bishop pointed to a spot. 'That's
where I fell in the dog's shit,' he declared, then returned to
the car, saying he would search no further. Swan and
Wilkinson examined the triangle of grass, 'but there was
nothing of note'. Bishop was taken to John Street police
station, where he arrived shortly after 11.15 a.m., to be
interviewed by Swan and Wilkinson in an office on the
first floor. They went through each statement, carefully
discussing the various points as they arose. Then a telephone rang and Swan left the room. He returned at 11.33
a.m. and said: 'As a result of what I have been told, I'm
arresting you for the murder of Nicola Fellows and Karen
Hadaway.' Bishop was cautioned and replied: 'No, no, it's
not me, fuck off, leave me alone, leave it out!'

Bishop was next interviewed in the cell block, with
Swan asking the questions and Wilkinson taking down
the interview in longhand, writing every word uttered by
both. The interview began at 1.46 p.m. Swan cautioned
the suspect and reminded him:

'You have been arrested for the murder of Nicola Fellows and Karen Hadaway. What have you got to say?'

'Not guilty.'

In the course of questioning, Bishop maintained that he had arrived home at about 6.15 p.m.

'I put the immersion on and got everything ready to do the washing, and sat down to watch EastEnders.'

'Why did you do the washing?'

'Because Jennie and myself had a row some weeks before about how the washing was done and we do our own washing ourselves. Mine needed doing.'

'What were you wearing that day?'

'Black shoes, white socks, blue jeans and a blue-grey jumper, I think.'

The questions continued until 2.22 p.m.

Bishop was taken to Dr Richard Gray, a deputy police surgeon, and at 2.55 p.m. was given an examination. Bishop gave his date of birth and stated that his general practitioner was Dr Eadie. Bishop's past medical history consisted of recurrent dislocations of both right and left shoulders. He claimed that he rarely drank but occasionally smoked cannabis; he also smoked twenty cigarettes a day. Bishop was measured at 5 foot 5 inches in height and 10 stone 5 pounds in weight. His hair was fair in colour, natural, with no parting; his eyes were blue. There was no nystagmus (involuntary movement of the eyeball) and the corneas were clear. Examination of the conjunctivae proved them normal; the pupils were equal, and responded to light and accommodation (close and longer focus). He had normal colour vision and did not wear spectacles or contact lenses.

Gray continued his examination and noted no abnormalities in Bishop's cardio-vascular system, respiratory system, alimentary system or central nervous system.

There was no evidence of mental illness and no evidence of hallucination or confabulation (a state of mind in which the gaps left by a disorder of the memory are replaced with imaginary-remembered experiences consistently believed to be true, a state also known as paramnesia).

Gray then concentrated on Bishop's breath and tongue; there was no odour and his tongue was clean, but he did have infected acne lesions round the mouth and chin. There was an old abrasion an inch and a half in length across the back of the left shoulder, three old abrasions on the back of the right hand, and a small three-quarter-inch abrasion at the base of the left-hand index finger. There were no other marks of trauma.

Police Superintendent Richard Flenley, superintendent of police responsible for support services in the Brighton police area, which includes the custody and welfare of prisoners, had seen Bishop before the interview had begun to initiate his Custody Record. Number 4967/86, it related to the detention of Russell Bishop and showed that he had been arrested on suspicion of murder. Under the provisions of the Police and Criminal Evidence Act (PACE) 1984, Flenley had requested Bishop to consent to providing both intimate and non-intimate body samples. Bishop had agreed to provide both and, as a consequence, gave written consent by endorsing the Custody Record with his signature. Flenley dictated the wording and assisted Bishop with the spelling of some of the words with which he had experienced difficulty.

Bishop then gave various body samples: saliva, anti-coagulated blood, blood for grouping and to be tested for drugs and alcohol, cut pubic hair, cut moustache hair, cut head hair, combed head hair and combed pubic hair. (Bishop refused an examination of his buttocks and inner thighs.)

At 10.30 a.m. on the 31st, after Bishop had been driven off by Swan and Wilkinson, DC Barry Evans and PC David Edwards had visited Jennie Johnson to show her the sealed 'Pinto' sweatshirt. As she was taking them into the lounge, she said, 'Oh, you've brought Russell's jumper back.'

Evans replied, 'This isn't one of those we took away.'

She asked, 'Where did you get it from then?'

Evans then asked, 'Is it Russell's?', pointing in the direction of the 'Pinto' which was now, in its bag, on the settee. She did not examine it but replied, 'Yes, he's got one exactly like it.' The sweatshirt was then moved to the floor.

'How long has he had it?'

'Some while, I don't remember.'

'It's got a motif on the front. Can you tell me if Russell's had one?'

'Yes, it's a name which begins with "P" or something.'

'Can we look in the wardrobe to see if Russell's is there?'

A search was made of the bedroom and the wardrobe, then Johnson remarked, 'I'll tell you what Russell has got on his, that's some red on one of his sleeves. It's where he was rubbing down one of his cars, it's compound or something. I've got some trousers of his with it on.'

She then gave Evans a pair of light blue trousers, badly worn and torn, which Edwards labelled JNJ/1.

Evans went on to ask, 'Where did Russell get the jumper from?'

'I don't know, he's had it for ages.'

'Can you remember if Russell wore it on Thursday, 9 October 1986?'

'No, I can't remember now.'

She then wrote a statement, or, to be precise, DC 889 Barry Evans wrote it down at her dictation: 'Further to my previous statement. On Friday, 31 October 1986 I was visited by Detective Constable Evans and Police Constable Edwards when I was shown a light blue sweatshirt. I recognised the sweatshirt as one exactly the same that Russell had. I recall that Russell had a motif on the front of his sweatshirt which was a name beginning with the letter "P".

'I did not examine the sweatshirt shown to me but can say that the one that Russell had had some red compound substance on one of the sleeves. I do not recall which sleeve. This substance had got on the jumper whilst Russell had been rubbing down one of his vehicles.

'I particularly recall the substance being there as it would never wash off. He also has the same substance on a pair of light blue trousers which I produce, labelled JNJ/1. I do not recall the last time I saw Russell's ~~jumper~~ [Johnson's correction] sweatshirt in the wardrobe but I cannot find the sweatshirt that Russell had.

'Russell has not told me that he did anything with the sweatshirt. I recently threw out some of Russell's, mine and our baby's clothes but I do not remember the sweatshirt being amongst those that have been thrown out.

'The sweatshirt that Russell owned was only latterly used by him as an item of work clothing and not something he would wear normally. Signed J. Johnson.'

It seems that the police officers carried out their questioning of Jennie Johnson in a straightforward and honest manner, though they always insist on writing statements out themselves, even when the witness is quite capable of doing it. In addition, and perhaps more importantly, the idea behind the written statement is to get down on paper an account of the events that police are enquiring into, and is inevitably a series of responses to leading questions. In this case the questions might have been, 'Have you seen this sweatshirt before?' or 'When did you last see this sweatshirt?' or 'Could you have thrown Russell's sweatshirt away?'

The police are ambiguous in their description of materials and substances. Gold is always called 'yellow metal' and silver 'white metal'. Any liquid or substance is normally called 'compound', hence the red paint became red compound. The interesting point is that the red compound actually was a substance termed 'rubbing down compound' and is used in the preparation of motor vehicles for paint spraying. Johnson, of course, went on to volunteer that Bishop had got the substance on his sweatshirt when rubbing down one of his motor vehicles, something the police had yet to learn about. Again, the claim that the substance would not wash off could hardly have been prompted by the police. Her final remark suggests that Bishop only wore the sweatshirt as an item of work clothing, indicating that originally he had used the garment for casual social wear, that it had been relegated to work clothing through age: 'He's had it for ages.' Her very first words, 'Oh, you've brought Russell's jumper back,' indicated that she believed she recognised the garment.

Having submitted himself for medical examination, Bishop was interviewed again at 3.38 p.m. He was reminded of the initial police caution and asked,

'Where are the clothes you wore on 9 October?'

'You've got them.'

'All of them?'

'Apart from my socks and my clothes on Friday, as well.'

'There's some indication that the top you wore had a round neck. Could that be true?'

'No, I don't think I've got a round-necked jumper. I think that's definitely the jumper you've got.'

'Have you ever owned a round-necked blue sweatshirt?'

Bishop then admitted that he did own a black round-necked sweatshirt. D S Swan continued:

'Jennifer seems to think you own a light blue one.'

'No, I've never had a light blue one. I've got a light blue jumper but it's a "V" neck.'

'Have you ever owned a light blue one?'

'Not light blue.'

'With the name "Pinto" on the chest?'

'No.'

'Jennifer says you have.'

'No.'

Swan then left the room and returned carrying the 'Pinto' sweatshirt which had now mysteriously changed its label back to the original REG/1.

'Is this your jumper?'

'No.'

Definitely no? Think hard, have a good look.'

The sweatshirt was thrown towards Bishop, who pushed it away.

'Definitely no. I've got a black one like that, not a blue one.'

'This morning Jennifer took police officers at their request to your wardrobe where she said there should be a blue "Pinto" sweatshirt. It was missing.'

D S Swan's remark was not strictly correct, as Johnson had referred only to a garment with a name beginning with 'P'.

'No.'

'Is this it?'

'No, I haven't got a blue sweatshirt.'

'Have you ever owned one?'

'Not one like that.'

'Not like this one? In your wardrobe was a pair of trousers that you had used for doing body repairs, rubbing down etc, on your car.'

'My grey ones.'

'Do you agree?'

'Yes.'

'On those trousers are red marks that won't come out. There may be marks on there [indicating the chest of the sweatshirt]. She says you had a similar red mark on your "Pinto" sweatshirt.'

Again, Swan was putting words into Jennie Johnson's mouth.

'No, she is mistaken.'

'She said it was on the cuff. Is that correct?'

Once again, Swan was misinforming Bishop of Johnson's claim. She referred to the sleeve only, not the cuff, and could not remember which sleeve.

'I haven't owned a jumper like this.'

Here Bishop contradicted himself. Moments before he claimed to have owned a black garment similar to the blue 'Pinto'.

'She told us this before she saw the jumper.'

Swan had perhaps forgotten or was not told that Johnson had seen the 'Pinto' as soon as the officers had walked through the door.

Bishop curtly replied, 'I don't think so.'

'And in fact when we showed the jumper to her she identified it as yours.'

'I've never had a jumper like that. She is mistaken for the black one.'

'As being yours because of the red on the cuff. Look at it.'

'I've never owned a jumper like that in my life.'

'So she guessed that my colleagues had a blue "Pinto" jumper with a red mark on the cuff before they'd mentioned it to her?'

Bishop would not change his mind. 'That's all I've got to say.'

'The red mark on your grey trousers – where did that come from?'

'My red Escort.'

'Where is the Escort?'

'Scrapped.'

'Where?'

'I don't know the name. I got it from the *Argus*.'

'What is the red mark?'

'Paint.'

This interview was terminated at 3.55 p.m. Bishop at first declined the offer to read the notes but he was asked again and agreed. Taking the bundle, he attempted to read every word. Being partially dyslexic, it wasn't surprising that he could understand very little of what he saw. He declined to sign the notes.

The 'Pinto' was handed back to Detective Inspector Chris Bentham. Its label was once again DE/1. Bentham says: 'About 3.50 p.m. the same day I was in the security area at Brighton police station when DS Swan returned the sweatshirt DE/1 to my possession. At 3.55 p.m. that day I handed this sweatshirt which was still in its sealed container to PC Lee, together with other articles, for conveyance to the Home Office Forensic Science Laboratory at Aldermaston.'

This garment had its label altered from REG/1 to DE/2 to REG/1 to DE/1 within the course of several weeks. At one point the label was lost altogether and frantic telephone calls were made to various officers to re-establish its origin and finder.

Russell Bishop was locked into a security cell and after supper, consisting of some rather cold fish and chips from the police canteen, he was interviewed once again, this time in the presence of Mr Oxford, a duty solicitor's clerk.

DS Swan began by trying to ascertain whether Bishop could read or write. It soon transpired that Bishop could not read at all well. Soon Swan reverted to the tactics he had employed earlier that afternoon. He told Bishop, 'I explained that before seeing your wife, Jennifer described to the police officers your clothes. One item in particular she describes as a blue sweatshirt with the word "Pinto" on the breast and she went on to say that it had a red mark on one of the cuffs. She said that you had got this on your jumper and also a pair of trousers whilst working on your car. You have told us that you have a pair of grey trousers with paint on them. Is that correct?'

'Yes,' he answered.

'She was then shown the jumper after she searched your wardrobe and couldn't find it and she is positive that the jumper we have is yours.'

'She is mistaken for another jumper which you have got already.'

'If the Forensic Science Laboratory say that the stains on the trousers and that jumper are from an identical source, what will your answer be?'

Bishop replied, 'No comment,' possibly the most sensible response he had made that day.

'We spoke about this at length this afternoon and one thing that I find strange, you have never once asked where we got the jumper from.'

'Okay, then,' replied Bishop. 'Where did you get it anyway?'

DS Swan immediately changed tack and began questioning Bishop about his movements earlier on the afternoon of 9 October. The interview was concluded at 8.52 p.m.

A police officer once explained: 'There are just three answers to give a questioning officer: "Yes, No and I don't know." To say any more if you are guilty of an offence means you are in trouble.' To an individual who has been in police custody prior to questioning, it can be a very frightening experience, more so if it is the first time. The prospect of being isolated in unfamiliar surroundings, treated as a criminal and possibly alienated from one's friends can be a daunting prospect. Bishop was the target of years of combined experience in interrogation technique, yet he would not change his mind over denying ownership of the blue 'Pinto' sweatshirt.

At 9.50 p.m. Bishop was escorted to his home, handcuffed to DC Wilkinson, who was in possession of a search warrant, and accompanied by Mr Oxford and by scenes of crimes investigators Redman, Fenner and Baynes, together with DC Payne. The officers searched the wardrobe, ignoring some of Bishop's clothes. Oxford wasn't satisfied and looked again through the wardrobe himself. He dug out a light blue short-sleeved summer shirt and a navy blue or black sweatshirt with a red motif on the left breast in the form of an initial 'P'. They went on to look at paint, and documents relating to Bishop's motor

KAREN JANE MICHELLE HADAWAY
BORN 21ST DECEMBER 1976
DIED 9TH OCTOBER 1986

NICOLA ELIZABETH CHRISTINE FELLOWS
BORN 22ND FEBRUARY 1977
DIED 9TH OCTOBER 1986

Christopher Berry-Dee by the graves of Karen Hadaway and Nicola Fellows

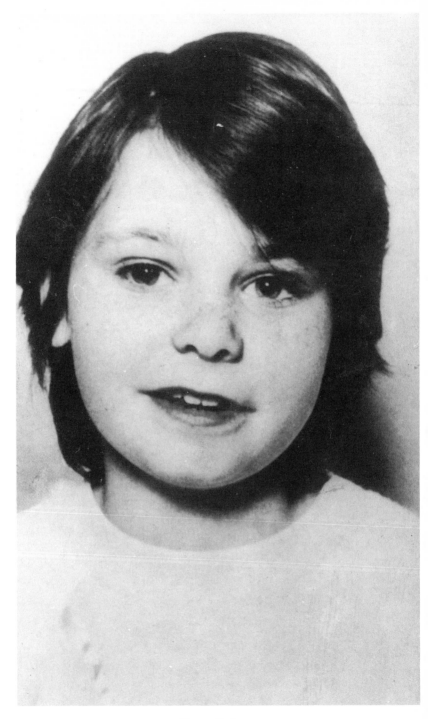

Karen Hadaway

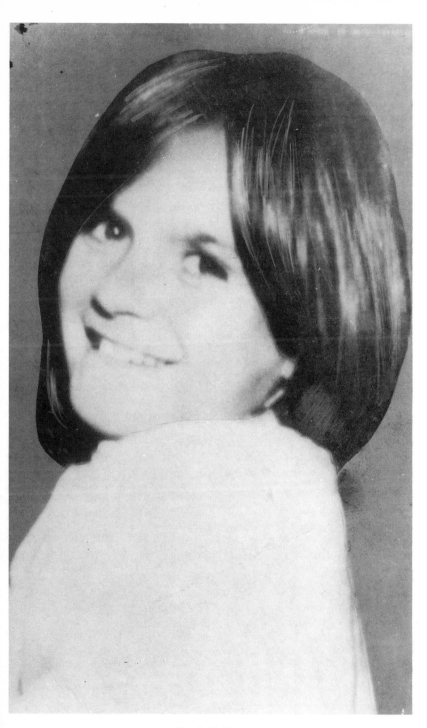

Nicola Fellows

Above: The Wild Park, showing where the girls' bodies were found (marked with an 'X' – the dots show the route of the footpath)

Below: The tree Karen and Nicola were seen swinging on shortly before their deaths on 9 October 1986

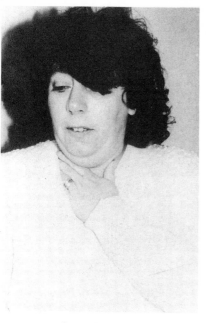

Susan Fellows

Barrie Fellows

Michelle and Lee Hadaway

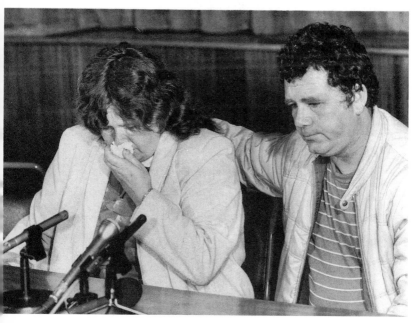

Above left: Marion Stevens

Above right: Jennie Johnson

Left: Russell Bishop

Above: The funeral on 4 February 1987

Right: Russell Bishop taking part in the protest march on 19 August 1989, campaigning to have the Babes in the Wood case re-opened

M U R D E R

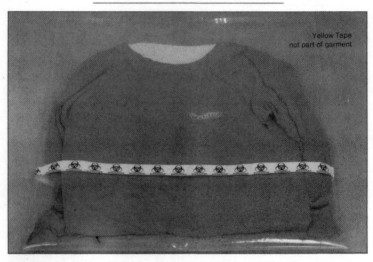

Yellow Tape
not part of garment

This really concerns every one of you – please give us your support on the 19th August. Meeting at the Wild Park (12 noon) then marching to John Street Police Station. Banners proposing to re-open the case will be welcome. This will be a peaceful march – please don't let us down.
Councillor Gordon J. Wingate, 27a Grove Street, Brighton BN2 2NY

On the 9th October 1986, Karen Hadaway and Nicola Fellows both aged nine years were taken to a lonely spot in the Wild Park, Moulsecoomb, Brighton. Both young girls were sexually assaulted then strangled by a person who they knew and trusted. That perverted killer is still at large today and could strike again.

It has been accepted by the Police and Forensic Scientists that this monster wore a blue sweatshirt. It is pale blue with the motif 'PINTO' emblazoned on the chest. It is a 42" chest.

Information has been provided that indicates who wore this garment and the details have been supplied to the Sussex Constabulary.

Karen and Nicola knew nothing of over-stretched police resources, or political implications. They did not understand deceit or down-right lying, they only understood a child-like innocence in the world they lived in. We as a Community owe it to their memories to bring this evil man to justice.

A second terrible injustice happened when Mr Russell Bishop was accused of these terrible crimes. He was totally innocent. It is the God given duty of the public to help locate this killer, the man who wore the Pinto sweatshirt. Some of you may know him and have seen him wearing this garment. It was discarded on the night of the killings the 9th/10th October 1986. It was found the following day.

IF YOU RECOGNISE THIS GARMENT AND HAVE SEEN SOMEONE IN THE PAST WEARING IT PLEASE CONTACT COUNCILLOR GORDON WINGATE, 27a GROVE STREET, BRIGHTON or c/o BRIGHTON TOWN HALL in complete confidence.

Remember that two little girls lie buried in Bear Road Cemetery, they could have been your children.

YOUR INFORMATION MIGHT BRING THIS KILLER TO JUSTICE.

From the Campaigners for Natural Justice for Nicola and Karen.

The first murder 'Wanted' poster in British criminal history

vehicles. Redman took possession of: EWR/64, clear plastic wallet containing torn photographs; EWR/65, vehicle document for a Datsun, index number VPN 197 S; EWR/66, 'Big Value' shopping pad; EWR/68, seven letters in a grey handbag found in a larder cupboard; EWR/69; handwritten receipt for a Ford Cortina, index number XMC 403 T; and EWR/70, quantity of torn photographs.

He then turned his attention to the outhouse, where he recorded details from a tin of Valentine's Spraygloss (Venetian Red) 178–40147 MNM 74308; the tin was in new condition and un-opened. Back at the larder, Redman found a spray gun and, returning to the outhouse, he saw a tin of 'Turtle Wax' car polish. He did not take any of these three items, but Payne confiscated a tin of Red Oxide. Fenner unearthed a tin of cellulose paint, which he removed, and Baynes found a grey jacket, which was left behind.

Redman now had to try to prove a link between the 'Pinto' sweatshirt and Bishop. He felt he could achieve this using the paint sample found on the sweatshirt and comparing it with paint from Bishop's car but, in order to do so, he had to track this vehicle down.

At midday on 25 October, John Hazel, a dealer in scrapped vehicles, had received a telephone call from Bishop saying that his Escort had 'blown' its engine and that Hazel could have the car for £40. Hazel had arrived at Bishop's home in Stephen's Road at 1.30 p.m. and went with Bishop to his car, still parked where he had abandoned it. After the usual haggling, a price was settled at £30. This was handed over in cash and Hazel received a handwritten receipt in exchange for the car. Over the coming weeks, Hazel dismantled the vehicle and sold various parts to customers. He eventually received a visit from Redman, who removed several samples of paint from a wing mirror, a right-side door and from the inside of the same door.

Before this happened, however, Bishop had been released on bail. He had been released from his cell by the jailer, Laurence Wickens, and taken to the custody sergeant who overheard Mr Oxford say, 'Can you make it clear that you have been treated well and fairly whilst you have been in police custody here?'

Bishop replied, 'Yes, I have.'

Oxford went on to suggest that Bishop should thank the superintendent, which he did reluctantly, shouting across his shoulder, 'Thanks, guv.' Bishop entered the Charge Room where he was bailed by Police Sergeant Hilliard in accordance with S47/3(B) of the Police and Criminal Evidence Act 1984. He was to return to the police station at 10.30 a.m. on Thursday, 4 December. He had been held in custody for a total of 51 hours: the detectives had had to apply to a magistrate for a warrant under the PACE Act to allow them to hold him for that period.

Bishop's bail began at 2.25 p.m. on 2 November 1986. He was driven to a secret London address by his solicitor, Ralph Haeems, in a brown Mercedes limousine.

7. Community Spirit

In the Moulsecoomb Estate, enquiries and interviews were being carried out on a previously unprecedented scale. The conviction grew that it was a local man who had killed the two girls and the search went inexorably from house to house. It was a slow process for the hundreds of police officers involved and, as might be expected, proved rather unsettling for a number of Moulsecoomb residents. Stolen property was hastily pushed out of sight; black and white television sets were placed where unlicensed colour sets had previously been; un-taxed motor vehicles were moved from outside homes and parked miles away. The enquiry was like piecing together a giant jig-saw puzzle of people's movements and observations without a clear idea of what would emerge. A killer was at large and had to be sought out.

The respectable Gray family, for instance, were knocked up early when the enquiries began at breakfast time; they were still in their nightclothes. They made PC Bob Hatley welcome with a cup of tea, as the *Evening Argus* reported, and after that he, together with 140 other uniformed police, worked untiringly through until dusk. Sixty of these officers were from Brighton, the remainder brought in from the various sub-divisions; the officer in charge, Inspector John Rodway, was normally assigned to licensing and drugs. Using two Portakabins placed side by side at the Moulsecoomb police box, he set up a temporary on-site headquarters. On the walls were lists of roads and names to be checked off. It was claimed that over 1,544 messages had been received by the police at their Incident Room, and every one had to be checked out. The *Argus* reported that a total of some 620 officers had been involved and some 7000 man-hours of police time taken up. Many police with children gave up their spare time to help find the killer.

The Brighton taxi drivers also joined the hunt, using their illuminated display signs to appeal for witnesses to come forward. That of Keith Machan, 29 and a father of three, read: 'MURDER ENQUIRY. Were you in the Wild Park or Moulsecoomb on 9 October? Contact Police 692136.' The illuminated signs had only been introduced in Brighton a month beforehand. Timothy Bridgnell, the boss of the 'Streamline' taxi company and also a father, said: 'The signs came with blank sheets of paper which could be inserted to show any special message to help police. This is the first time we have had to use them for a very sad reason.'

Two *Argus* reporters, Jim Hatley and Jim Wells, confronted the police, requesting information for release over the following days. A computer incident room had been organised at Brighton police station and officers contacted other murder teams investigating the killing of young girls around Britain. The police chiefs had issued a fresh appeal for information. Inspector Peter Kennett said, 'We are looking for a vicious, callous murderer.' Then he issued a grim warning to all parents: 'There is someone out there who has killed two young girls and there is always the possibility that he could do it again. It would be very wise for parents to know where their children are at all times.'

David Barnard, chairman of the East Moulsecoomb

Residents' Association, made the following statement: 'There are no children on the streets today. Parents can hardly bear to let them out of their sight for a minute, let alone outside to play.' He continued, '. . . The estate is very quiet and shocked. Parents here have been worried about their children for some time now. But how do you protect them from things like this?' Unable to resist a slap at the local authorities, he argued, 'There is a lack of play facilities. The children have been forced to play on the streets.'

It had not taken more than a few hours for the local authorities to come under attack; the safety of Brighton's parks had to be discussed at an emergency meeting on Saturday, 11 October. The meeting was called by Councillor Brian Fitch, chairman of the Parks and Recreation Committee. Mr Michael Griffen, the department's director, and the superintendent of the park's police were to be present. On the agenda was a proposal that would involve employment of 'Park Rangers' equipped with radios and Land Rovers, who would be in contact with the park police. The initial cost would be about £50,000. Some of the cash, Fitch claimed, might come from the Countryside Commission. Other suggestions included ways of improving the park police shift system to ensure greater coverage – this in the realisation that the murders had occurred just 50 yards from a police box. Fitch admitted, however, that no matter how many park police were employed it would be impossible to ensure that places such as the Wild Park were 100 per cent safe.

A further meeting was to be held on the following Monday. One individual came up with an idea which in itself was generous and typical of a caring community. Kenneth Parker of Eggington Road organised a Reward Fund for the capture of the killer and within hours had raised

almost £800 from his business associates in the antiques
trade. Russell Bishop's uncle, an antique dealer with
premises in the Lanes in Brighton, contributed. The
Hiker's Rest pub in Coldean Lane pledged its support, one
customer claiming: 'Ordinary blokes vowed to give £100.
Everyone is really bitter and if we get our hands on who-
ever did it before the police do, they will be mincemeat.'
Colin Bradford, Chairman of the North Moulsecoomb
Residents' Association, started up a commemorative
Charity Fund to raise money for a local hospital; he
donated £25 and placed a collection box in the Barcombe
Road post office.

On Sunday a church service was held for the dead girls.
The Moulsecoomb priest, the Reverend Michael Porteous,
appealed for calm in a community hell-bent on revenge.
He told the weeping congregation, 'Ease the hatred from
your hearts,' begging them to pray for the brutal killer
who had sexually assaulted the girls before slaying them.
Even as he spoke, he confessed to himself that his words
could be falling upon deaf ears. He was right. Supporting
the two families, who had probably not been inside a
church more than a handful of times in their lives, was a
remarkable turnout. Over 60 people packed themselves
inside the tiny building. The man now leading the murder
hunt, head of Sussex CID, Detective Chief Superintendent John McConnell, took time out from the enquiry
to share in the community's grief. The Church Army
Captain, Jim Wilson, attended and said a few words. The
church was charged with emotion as he echoed the fears
of an estate rocked with revulsion and shock. The congregation stood with heads bowed as children laid posies on
the altar. Music from Fauré's 'Pavanne' played over the
speakers, then the church became silent as Reverend

Porteous climbed the steps to lead prayers. As friends of the children wept, he said, 'We are bewildered by the evil and violence that caused these deaths. We now pray for Karen and Nicola, sure in the hope that God has taken them to Him. They are at one with Him in that place where there is no more weeping or sighing. Grant them eternal rest and may perpetual light shine on them forever.'

Outside the Holy Nativity Church 37-year-old Angela Cork sobbed when she remembered Karen as a sweet, lovely little girl. She used to baby-sit for the Hadaways, and her nephew, eleven-year-old Mark, had been one of Karen's playmates. The young lad had already run home, sobbing hysterically. Thinking about the priest's pleas for mercy, she said, 'If I saw the man who did this now, I would probably strangle him with my bare hands.'

The congregation filed slowly out into the sunshine. The church was empty again. All but for one little person. A schoolfriend of Karen's wanted to stay. She moved quietly out of her pew and walked towards the altar where, without fuss, she knelt down on one knee. After placing a posy specially selected by her mother, the girl prayed. Then she took from her pocket a clean white handkerchief, freshly ironed, and burst into uncontrollable tears.

William Cutting, the stepfather of Matthew Marchant, one of the young men who had found the bodies, described Nicola as a lovely, affectionate girl. 'She would come up to you and throw her arms around you to give you a cuddle. I cried my eyes out when I heard the news.' But his grief was tinged with the same bitter anger that had spread throughout the estate. 'If I found the person who did this I would carve him up without a second thought. I may go to prison for life, but I would enjoy killing him, enjoy doing it.' The local postmaster, Tom

Blackburn, summarised the feelings of his rough community: 'The people are sure someone round here got
these two children and they want blood for it.' PC Eric
McIntosh, who had been the local beat officer, tried inef-
fectively to pour oil on the boiling waters. He, too, knew
Nicola and said, 'She was a kid who would come up to you
in the street and hold your hand.' He went on, 'However
hard it is round here, it is a community. They may have
scraps round here, but when they need each other they
are there.'

It was 5.30 p.m. on 16 October. The traffic queue had built
up and some of the drivers were becoming extremely
impatient: five hours was long enough to strain the
patience of any commuter who had to sit and wait in a
vehicle which was running hot and consuming extra fuel.
The A27 Brighton to Lewes road was jammed solid, with
both lanes brought to a crawl, and traffic tailing back to
the Grand Parade and Preston Circus. It was well after 10
p.m. before traffic was flowing normally. At a police road
block, murder enquiry detectives were asking every
driver and passenger, 'Did you see these two young girls
on the ninth of October at about six o'clock?' Eighteen
thousand people were asked that single question. More
than a hundred gave information which might prove
useful.

A Brighton transport spokesman said, 'It's absolutely
decimated our services. The schedules are all over the
place.' Southern Taxis reported that one journey from the
Royal Alexandra Hospital in Dyke Road to Moulsecoomb
had taken a record 88 minutes. But the public had
remained good-humoured despite suppers spoiled, cars
out of petrol and people being late for appointments and
evening classes. Driving instructor Roger Cole, who was

twenty minutes behind schedule, said, 'I haven't seen jams like this since the Grand Hotel bombing,' adding, 'I don't mind waiting since there is a good reason.' Police used loud-hailers to speak to bus passengers. One delighted bus driver shouted down from his cab: 'I'm on overtime. If I'd known about this then, I might have finished earlier, but the extra cash will keep the old lady sweet.'

As the day drew on, however, several parents became concerned about their children, late home from school, and began to telephone the bus company – for instance when the 3.23 p.m. failed to turn up at the Margaret Hardy School for Girls. The driver had been given incorrect route instructions for the afternoon and the bus did not arrive at all, with the result that dozens of girls had to walk home through some rather unpleasant areas. A spokesman for the bus company, Martin Harris, said, 'We have to confess the driver is completely blameless. It is very unfortunate, particularly at this time, and we apologise profusely to all those affected.'

The BBC *Crimewatch* programme had screened Nicola and Karen's last walk, re-enacted in front of blazing lights and under the watchful eyes of parents and police. Plucky schoolgirls Lianne Martin and Katrina Taylor went through a two-hour ordeal impersonating their dead companions in a bid to trap a killer. It became too much for Barrie Fellows, who was led away in tears. As the light faded, detectives began to move in and questioned everyone in the vicinity again about their movements on the 9th. This ending was a happy one, though, for at the exact moment the victims were thought to have disappeared, the tired Lianne and Katrina were cuddled by their mothers and led to the warmth of their homes. One of them, shivering in the cold air, was wrapped in a police overcoat and given a police helmet for good measure.

After seeing the programme, *EastEnders* star Nick Berry (Wicksy the Barman) sent his record 'Every Loser Wins' to the Fellows household. It had been Nicola's favourite disc.

Not everyone appeared sympathetic to the bereaved families. Mrs Goldie Gardener, a local Tory councillor and former Eastbourne Mayor, blamed the parents for allowing their children out to play so late. Addressing an East Sussex Education Committee, she said simply, 'It was the responsibility of the parents.' Uproar and indignation ensued and it was left to a colleague, Mrs Beryl Thomas, chairman of the Schools Sub-Committee, to retrieve the situation.

'I have enormous and very sincere sympathy for the parents of the little girls and am disgusted with my colleague's remarks.' The fair-haired, chubby-faced Gardener retreated to the back of the room and the meeting ended in chaos. Mrs Thomas shouted at the top of her voice, in her attempts to minimise the damage, 'I am sure that the parents loved and cared for the children as I would do my own.' The Labour councillor, Brian Fitch, took a well-aimed shot at his Conservative counterpart. 'Never in my fourteen years as a councillor have I heard such a disgraceful and disgusting speech,' he said, his voice raised a full octave. 'She should be censored and removed.' He continued, 'To come out with those remarks about the parents who have suffered such a tragedy is both callous and cruel.' Councillor David Hill, the Labour leader, chimed in, 'To accuse the grieving parents of being responsible for their daughters' deaths is totally unacceptable. It shows how Mrs Gardener is totally out of touch. This community needs help, not a slap in the face.' Threats to send the lady to Coventry and to ostracise her politically echoed round the hall. Goldie Gardener had been a councillor in the Upperton ward for twenty years and was to all intents and purposes a strong and well-respected member of the Tory community.

Another heated row broke out almost immediately. Soon Labour and Alliance members joined forces and proposed that extra money should be found to employ another worker at St George's Hall in Newick Road. It was a way of keeping the children off the streets, they suggested, and asked for £2700 to employ a person from January. Councillor Fitch rose once again to join battle, calling the Tories of East Sussex 'skinflints'.

The neighbourhood started a petition calling for the re-introduction of capital punishment. No doubt there were those who hoped Mrs Gardener might become the hangman's first victim, with the remainder of the Tory party qualifying for sentencing forthwith.

Many people did more than just talk, of course. Deep in the Sussex countryside, Mrs Eugenia Bowery of Gillingham Close, Horsham, was busy at her kiln making hundreds of ceramic tags for children, each bearing a secret code sign. She told reporters from the *Evening Argus*: 'The parents would have an identical copy. It would stop children going with strangers: if the parents sent anyone to pick them up they should give them the tag so the children know they are safe.'

On Saturday, 11 October, DC Gibbon had helped Lee Hadaway and Barrie Fellows to identify their daughters at the borough mortuary, but the East Sussex coroner, Dr Donald Wooding, could not release the bodies for burial. With no final act of that kind, and with police enquiries continuing round the clock, there was no possibility for friends and families to begin the process of recovery from bereavement.

An uncanny stillness had descended over the Moulsecoomb Estate. It seemed as if the pressure that had been
building up over the previous weeks had evaporated with
the arrest of Russell Bishop on 31 October. Of course,
there was the never-ending gossip, the rounds of neighbours, tittle-tattling from door to door. Venomous back-
stabbing provided the main topic of conversation in the
bar of the Hiker's Rest and anyone who had anything to
do with Russell Bishop became the target for abuse.
Hushed, backs-turned conversation ensued when someone strolled past. 'Oh, him. Well, of course, my hubby
always reckoned that they knew far more than they let
on. Mrs So-and-so said the very same thing the other day.'
The estate thrived on such scandal, for it provided the
bored inhabitants with tasty morsels of excitement that
saw them through another day. News, it seemed, travel-
led across garden fences faster than by telephone.

Many people in Moulsecoomb, with their wagging
tongues, ignorant and stupid, turned against Marion
Stevenson and her totally innocent family. She became
fearful for her safety. 'Every time I go out with my
parents, I feel frightened for them. It's so unfair. What the
hell have they done? What has my family done? It doesn't
make sense.'

Jim Stevenson, Marion's father, is a powerfully built
Scot. Forty-five and partially disabled, he is as honest as
the day is long and makes the best cup of tea west of
Eastbourne. He idolises Marion but did not approve of her
seeing Bishop, as she had been doing for some eight
months. Rosalind, his wife, works for American Express
as a cleaner. She is a nervous woman and has a heart of
gold.

As the weeks passed, the family began to suffer from a
stream of abuse directed at their front door. They had

always dreamed of leaving Moulsecoomb when those elusive funds became available, but now they were ostracised by their community with veiled threats and malicious gossip. Jim Stevenson reflected, 'I can hardly afford to move but maybe now I'll have to. It's like living on a timebomb. Every noise I hear in the night, I wonder if there's some maniac outside looking for trouble. There are painful memories for us here – but then people would think we are running away from everything. It's funny. We could have made thousands of pounds out of this, national newspapers were offering us the earth, but I just don't think it is right to profit out of something so tragic as this. There is a lot of good in Moulsecoomb. Unfortunately, there is a bad and sinister element, which rather taints the estate.'

Jim and Rosalind Stevenson stuck it out and for doing so may well hold their heads up with pride. The community should respect that; I certainly do.

Other men were unwittingly thrust into the public spotlight, rumour wrongly accusing them of a heartless con-trick. Nigel Kinsy, aged eighteen, and Scott Green, seventeen, had spent an entire weekend working hard collecting for the Appeal Fund. Suddenly they were targets for claims that two teenagers collecting on the estate were working for a 'Fagin-type' character. But with £600 in their collection boxes ready for banking, they were clearly doing a grand and charitable job and the rumours were soon scotched.

Elsewhere, sticky fingers *had* been in the till. Thirty-year-old Kenneth Bass, an immediate neighbour of the bereaved families, decided that the Appeal Fund might well provide a welcome supplement to his own meagre income from Social Security. Full-faced under a tousled mop of unkempt, greasy hair, Bass was lucky ever to see his shoes, hidden by a beer-belly. His wife, Lynda, a hard-faced woman, was the less dominant of the pair. For a period they were in charge of the Appeal Fund and temptation became too much. At first they extracted just a few pounds. Ken Bass was now in the pub more often, hoping to gain the respect of the few drinking partners he could muster. Then their home began to boast one or two of the more extravagant luxuries in life, and soon the gossip began. After a while the Fund's records and receipts were checked by a self-policing body of residents and were found to be £700 light. The Basses were charged with theft and brought before the Brighton Bench but, released on unconditional bail, they fled from justice. Lynda has now returned to England where she was arrested by police and sentenced to six months' imprisonment; the judge at her trial described her as a mean and deceitful woman. At the time of writing, Kenneth Bass is still a fugitive.

The Fund continued to grow. On the afternoon of 30 November 1986 it grew by £5000, delivered by its donor, who arrived in a gleaming blue Rolls-Royce. The generous benefactor, a millionaire Muslim leader, R. Shamsudin Alfasi, pulled up outside the Hadaways' home. Surrounded by burly bodyguards, he stayed for a few minutes, posing for photographs, before speeding off to the Grand Hotel where he intended to stay the night. Ten minutes later another gift arrived. A ten-year-old girl tapped nervously on the Hadaways' door. She had saved just £1 from her pocket money. She was rewarded with a hug and a kiss.

Four other schoolgirls, from St Peter's School, Cowfold, recorded a song, 'Say No To Strangers', set to a tune from the BBC's *Grange Hill*. Their teacher, Sally Wilton, chose the title.

'Don't go in anyone else's car unless it's someone you
know.
   Just say NO.
Don't take sweets from anyone, just your mum.
   Just say NO.
All you children, you'd better watch out, bad people
about,
   Bad people about, watch out.
Just say NO. NO. Just say NO.
   Don't go with anyone you don't know.'

Sensible and well-intentioned advice, with perhaps a
lingering innocence in its last line.

The national police computer in London had been linked
to Brighton; far from scaling down the hunt, the Sussex
police had scaled it up. Another twenty experienced
detectives had joined the team on 25 October; the murder
squad now numbered 75 men and women, with a further
45 in the incident room. There were several issues that the
investigating officers were trying to resolve. A CB radio
user with the call-sign 'Whispering Willie' had boasted
over the air of killing the girls, but the police believed he
was just a callous hoaxer. There was also the driver of a
maroon-coloured car seen leaving the Wild Park on the
evening the girls disappeared, who had not come forward
to eliminate himself from the enquiry. In addition, two
youths had been seen running from the Wild Park across
Lewes Road into Moulsecoomb Estate on the evening of 9
October, and had not come forward to assist the police.
   The Member of Parliament for Brighton Kemp Town,
Andrew Bowden, had been in the United States when the
murders were committed, but as soon as he set foot in his
home town he paid a visit to Moulsecoomb, accompanied

by Detective Chief Superintendent John McConnell. Crossing Lewes Road flanked by several plain-clothes detective officers and uniformed men, McConnell explained that five witnesses had seen the two youths running across the dual-carriageway at that point. One of them had narrowly missed a car, which had swerved to avoid hitting him. Bowden listened and offered his total support.

There was another item outstanding, namely the blue 'Pinto' sweatshirt. Whoever dropped the garment had not claimed it, despite repeated requests to do so from the police.

8. Investigation

Within a few days of giving her statement that the blue 'Pinto' sweatshirt had belonged to Russell Bishop, Jennie Johnson claimed that the statement was a fabrication by the police in an attempt to 'fit up' Russell.

It is worth noting that the police had no idea of the value of the 'Pinto' in forensic terms when they first produced the sweatshirt to Johnson; it could have been anyone's sweatshirt. In this context, they had no reason to 'fit Bishop up' by concocting a false statement taken from her. It is also worth noting that Johnson did not alter her initial identification of the 'Pinto' in a further statement made to the police, but she changed her mind on 13 October 1987 in a statement to Ralph Haeems, Russell Bishop's lawyer.

Referring to the 'Pinto', she says: 'I was shown it at least six feet away but I couldn't positively identify it. It was never taken out of the bag, unfolded and shown to me. I am able to say with absolute certainty that I have never seen Russell wearing a sweatshirt of any colour with a motif by the name "Pinto" written on it. Russell has never owned such a shirt. I do not even recall seeing such a sweatshirt.' She went further, saying that she had never read the statements taken from her by the police and that she hadn't even signed them. Her signature, she claimed, had been forged. Clearly Jennie Johnson, as the trial judge later confirmed, is a self-confessed liar and perjurer. Her later statement hit the police like a bombshell: with no eye-witness statements worth their salt, they now had to rely on forensic evidence alone in their case against the man now out again in the community on bail.

On Saturday, 22 November 1986 an amazing incident took place at the Bishops' flat. It comes as no surprise to learn that Marion Stevenson was there while Jennie Johnson was out shopping in Brighton. Marion had walked up to Stephen's Road, arriving at about 3.30 p.m. Bishop claimed that while he had been waiting for her, a man had just broken into his electricity meter and escaped by jumping through a window. The police were called, but there were no witnesses and no one has been charged with this theft, least of all Bishop, who suddenly acquired money for a drink with Stevenson that night.

A blue sweatshirt had been lying across the fireguard. Bishop explained to Stevenson, 'That's the jumper I was on about and they haven't got the right one. I am going to make sure them [sic] lot don't get it as they would get me done for it.'

Bishop was referring to a sweatshirt he claimed he had been wearing on 9 October, with a thick white diagonal stripe across the chest and a thinner red stripe below it, the very same sweatshirt identified by Michelle Hadaway as being the garment worn by Bishop that day. This sweater had red paint on the left sleeve and a hole in the same sleeve and had apparently been left at Bishop's parents' home for some while. The police arrived to examine the electricity meter, were shown the sweater by Stevenson and took no notice of it.

In the investigations that followed and in the trial of Russell Bishop, several major issues were raised, issues that relate to the investigation of any crime of this kind, and relate also to prosecution and defence methods and means.

Before dealing with details of evidence and investigative conduct, it might be as well to consider the kind of criminal the police were searching for, whether or not the two girls knew their killer, and the manner of their death.

The evidence assembled against Russell Bishop can at best be described as circumstantial evidence and in its weakest form. There is rarely any suspect or detained individual whose previous character is totally above suspicion and whose recollections accord correctly with events. How much more fallible, then, is the evidence of a witness who is open to bias and ill-will and who is tempted to exaggerate or to lie from the outset.

It may be noted in favour of circumstantial evidence that proof is only 'excessive probability' of a kind so forceful as to eliminate all room for doubt. Convictions based on circumstantial evidence depend on the integrity of that evidence; on the cumulative effect of numerous factors which, in combination, defeat coincidence; on factors not in dispute being used to infer a factor that is. It is the cumulative effect which causes so many juries to say that even though the evidence before them is entirely indirect or circumstantial in nature, they are satisfied beyond any reasonable doubt of the safety of bringing in a guilty verdict.

A number of factors bearing on the behaviour of a suspect come into the reckoning when considering the value of circumstantial evidence. Three classic elements are motive, method and opportunity. Crimes are usually committed for some discernible reason; there may be evidence of preparation and intent before the crime was committed. There must be method, with all the scope this subsequently offers for scientific investigation; and there must be opportunity, that combination of movement and time that creates the right moment for a criminal to strike. In murder, the elements of opportunity are an equation between the movements of both victim and killer; the result may be an opportunity that is planned or one that is simply spontaneous, in the sense that it may be called opportunistic.

Other factors come into consideration after the crime has been committed. These include acts indicating guilty conscience or indirect admission of guilt; possession of fruits of the crime; refusal to account for suspicious activities; and tampering with or fabrication of evidence.

These factors are by no means exhaustive and it is not easy to classify circumstances by them. Usually, it is to motive that investigators look first. Motive may be described as the mental mainspring of a crime, but it should not be confused with intent: 'A man's motive may be good, but his intention bad.' A loaf is stolen. The intention was to steal and the act was therefore criminal although the motive, to save a starving child, was good. But in general, motive and intention are so entwined that it is difficult to separate them. The commonest forms of motive have been described by Christmas Humphreys in *Seven Murders* as 'the desire of avenging some real or fancied wrong; of escaping from the pressure of pecuniary or other obligation; of getting rid of a rival or obnoxious connection; of obtaining plunder or other coveted objects; of preserving reputation, or of gratifying some other selfish or malignant passion'. In the modern idiom these may be summed up more concisely as revenge, gain, elimination, conviction and lust.

What is certain is that proof of motive is never necessary to prove a crime. This is probably just as well, for the most brilliant jury is helpless at deciding the mental processes which drive a criminal. Where a motive is apparent, though, it is at least a factor to be taken into account. In the case of Russell Bishop, the question of motive is easily disposed of for there was nothing in October 1986, either known about his background or seen from his demeanour, to suggest a sexual lust that would lead him to murder two young girls.

Nor is there anything in this sad case that hints at guilty conscience, at intent or preparation on his part, although there were opportunities in abundance. Where opportunity can be proved alongside motive and method, *prima facie* evidence of guilt can be argued. Opportunity is also the positive aspect of the famous and much used negative, the alibi. If the accused person was demonstrably somewhere other than the scene of the crime at the time the offence was committed, he clearly lacked opportunity, even though there might be an apparently strong motive.

In Bishop's case, the evidence regarding his proximity to the scene of the crime was conflicting. He was seen on the day of the murders at 5.15 p.m. by Roy Dadswell, the Park Constable. Later, at about 6.15 p.m., he was seen walking along Lewes Road by two men on their way home from work. His direction at that time was taking him away from the crime scene. He was found at home in Stephen's Road by Jennie Johnson at some time before 9 p.m. He had been there long enough to take a bath and eat a small snack. The forensic pathologist gave the earliest time of death as 7 p.m.

There were no fruits of the crime to be found, or stolen property, and there was a total absence of any murder weapon, as the murderer or murderers had killed with bare hands.

Failure to give a satisfactory explanation of events is an

obvious indication for suspicion. An innocent person will presumably act in the manner expected of a person with nothing to conceal and will be only too anxious to explain at the earliest possible opportunity any apparently suspicious circumstances that have led to an accusation. Any unwillingness to explain suspicious circumstances is a factor to be considered in assessing a person's likely guilt. Similarly, any uncalled-for explanation, or excessive anxiety to explain what may not even be regarded as suspicious, might be viewed as not wholly compatible with innocence.

The main reason for Russell Bishop's arrest lay in his own ill-advised remarks. He lied about the purchase of drugs and an evening newspaper, and his comment that he had seen blood-flecked foam on Nicola Fellows' lips has never been adequately explained. He claimed that PCAS Smith mentioned this, but Smith denies it, as do Matthew Marchant and Kevin Rowland, who found the bodies.

With the withdrawal of Jennie Johnson's statement, she became a hostile witness and was of no use to the police. Indeed, the evidence against Bishop was so weak at the outset that one of the Brighton magistrates on the Bench for the committal hearing recently acknowledged that the Bench had experienced great difficulty in forming an opinion that Bishop should be sent for trial.

It is worthwhile pausing for a moment to compare Bishop's behaviour with that of the profiled sexual psychopath. The latter acts without creating suspicion, protected by native cunning and cool-headed enough to cover his tracks. Did Bishop take the two girls by chance, as did a recently convicted sexual psychopath, Colin Pitchfork, a sexual pervert, a flasher, who roamed the villages of Narborough and Littlethorpe in Leicestershire? He was jailed on 27 January 1988 for the murder of two young girls.

Another sexual psychopath, John David Guise Cannan, killed newly-wed Shirley Banks in 1987. Cannan committed many rapes and possibly killed estate agent Suzy Lamplugh. Both men happened across their victims by chance.

No psychopathic tendencies were noted in Bishop's character while he was on remand at Brixton and under the observation of the medical authorities. He had no history of abnormal sexual behaviour which might have manifested itself in the sexual abuse and killing of two young girls.

So what manner of man was he, this killer of two innocent children? If he *was* known to the girls, as seems likely, he might have sought to abuse them in a lesser way and keep his secret by coaxing or threatening them to stay silent. Recent sociological studies have shown that there are all too many sexual perverts operating within the family network in Britain, relying on innocence and ignorance to cloak their assaults.

The state of mind of the murderer or murderers can only be assessed by applying informed common sense to what is known about the crime. It is important to note that Nicola was very seriously sexually assaulted, which rather suggests that her killer was more attracted to her than to Karen. With uncontrollable emotions surging in the assailant's brain and becoming manifest in his behaviour, both girls panicked. The assault rapidly slipped out of the man's control and the only way he could escape and retain his anonymity was by killing them.

An even more sinister explanation is that the killer was a homicidal sexual psychopath, a person with a disordered mind, stimulated by violence and likely to kill again. The psychopath, the so-called 'cold-blooded killer' written about in the tabloid press, is difficult to define and even more difficult to identify.

In 1835 James Cowles Prichard, an English physician and one of the first Commissioners in Lunacy, described a type of madness which lacked the characteristics of insanity. He wrote about 'a morbid perversion of the natural feelings' accompanied by no observable disorder or defect. He was talking about the psychopathic condition in which an individual who is to all intents and purposes normal, and capable of distinguishing between good and evil, nevertheless acts without moral restraint. Victorians continued to talk about 'moral insanity', a condition which Prichard acknowledged was 'as numerous as the modifications of feelings or passion in the human mind'.

There was a surge of interest in the study of insanity in the 1840s, as doctors sought to explain and define the aberrant aspects of human behaviour. Dr John Connolly, a London practitioner, played a leading role in establishing what was to become, in 1865, the Medico-Psychological Association; prior to this, doctors who studied and treated mental disorders were known as alienists. Connolly pioneered a more scientific approach to the subject, describing individuals who were extremely 'selfish, cruel and alcoholic and prone to indulge in illegal activity such as fraud, forgery and even murder . . . perpetrated as a result of a sudden homicidal impulse'.

Connolly understood the significance of a long history of disordered behaviour as a prerequisite for diagnosing what today is called psychopathic disorder. His use of the term 'morbidly intense perception' was particularly interesting. Psychopaths are unduly vulnerable emotionally and often take unwarranted offence at the words, actions or attitudes of others. Their reactions to stress are frequently exaggerated and abnormal, owing to the strong feelings of inferiority and compensatory arrogance which exist side by side.

By the 1880s, a decade which acknowledged murder for sexual motives in the anonymous shape of Jack the Ripper, alienists had begun to recognise a condition that was not a psychosis and not due to insanity. The term 'psychopath' to describe this condition was first used in 1891 by a German doctor. The psychopathic personality is regarded as one of the greatest problems in forensic psychiatry. John B. Martin, in his book *Break Down The Walls*, gave a pen picture of the psychopath as a person whose emotions 'are out of kilter – he is cold, remote, indifferent to the plight of others, hostile even'. The American neuro-psychiatrist, Professor H. Cleckley, defined this type of personality as one who 'can perceive consequences, formulate in theory a wise course of conduct, name and phrase what is regarded as desirable or admirable; but his disorder is, apparently, such that he does not feel sufficiently about these things to be moved and to act accordingly'.

A murderer whose personality fitted this definition was Neville Heath, hanged in 1946 for killing two women with sadistic brutality. He was a social misfit, a plausible and intelligent man who disappointed his family and friends with his lack of effort to pursue a promising career. Heath was intolerant of discipline and social obligations, and developed cruel and anti-social traits which ended up with murder. He was a ladies' man whose appearance gave no hint of the violence and sexual perversion beneath the surface of his character.

It is this outward plausibility, often combined with an impressive personality, that so bewitches the psychopath's victims. Heath easily charmed his victims to death and a new generation of serial killers has since repeated

the formula. Peter Sutcliffe, the Yorkshire Ripper, murdered thirteen women and was tried for his crimes in
1981. The jury rejected his defence plea of insanity, as did
the jury at Heath's trial. Mr Justice Morris, summing up,
said '. . . you will see that insanity is not to be found
merely because some conduct might be regarded as so
outrageous as to be wholly unexpected from the gen-
erality of men. Strong sexual instinct is not of itself
insanity; a mere love of bloodshed, or mere recklessness,
are not in themselves insanity; an inability to resist temptation is not itself insanity; equally, the satisfaction of
some invented impulse is not, without more, to be
excused on the grounds of insanity.'

In general, psychopathic murderers on both sides of the
Atlantic, while they have frequently sought refuge in
pleas of insanity, have seldom succeeded. This comes
from the understanding that ordinary men and women
now have of psychopaths who demonstrate their
apparent normality so graphically in the sense that even
those closest to them – friends and family – are unaware
of their secret and perverted excesses. Dr Martin Blinder,
an American legal pyschiatrist, put it succinctly when he
wrote, 'The psychopath at first glance seems quite well
put together.' He went on to enumerate the qualities of
personality involved: 'There are no delusions or halluci-
nations, no memory loss and a solid grasp of reality. His
defects, the signs of wayward behaviour, are chronic inability to conform to social norms, to defer gratification,
tolerate frustration, control impulses or to form
relationships.

What drives the psychopath is the desire to take what
he wants regardless of the consequences. He is insensitive
to all but his own needs; his inability to recognise the
needs or rights of other human beings means that he

sweeps them casually aside or simply uses them for his own ends. Of course, not all individuals with psycho-pathic tendencies in their character commit murder, though they may at times be violent or extreme in their behaviour as an outlet for bottled-up emotions and inner tensions.

Psychopathic personalities have an essentially anti-social character usually originating in childhood. They suffer from feelings of deprivation which tend to alienate them from the rest of humanity, and they grow up as indi-viduals without a social conscience. Hence the psycho-path, described by one authority as the 'supreme con-artist', acts simply out of self-interest. The murderous psychopath is characterised by his lack of either guilt or remorse; lacking any inhibitions or restraints, such a per-son is likely to kill again and again. The mainspring for his killing is not mental disability, but to profit by grati-fication.

But for all his lack of social conscience, his disregard for the feelings of others, his inability to feel guilt and capacity for violence, the psychopath knows when he is commit-ting a wrongful act. He understands the rules by which society operates but elects to override them to satisfy his private passions. He is perverted but sane. His ethos is: 'I don't care – I'll have what I want.' Denis Nilsen, the mild-mannered civil servant who slaughtered fifteen young down-and-outs in London in the early 1980s, was such a person. Mr Justice Croom-Johnson said of him, 'A mind can be evil without being abnormal.' He added, 'There are evil people who do evil things. Committing murder is one of them.'

The Mental Health Act (1983) defines psychopathic dis-order as 'a persistent disorder or disability of mind, whether or not including significant impairment of intelligence, which results in abnormally aggressive or seriously irresponsible conduct'. Dr Denis Power, writing in *The Criminologist*, commented on the difficulties involved in attempting to define the psychopathic type. He emphasised that there was no objective test for any form of psychopathic disorder, but that there were a number of comparative criteria which distinguished the psychopath from the non-psychopath. Persistently abnormal behaviour was an important characteristic: a single anti-social act, no matter how violent it was, would not merit a psychopathic label. Inability to learn from experience was a behavioural trait in psychopaths, so that their bad conduct tended to be repeated and on an increasing scale of violence.

In general, the psychopath tends to be a person who carries out petty crimes when there is no material need and often makes scant use of his gains anyway. While acknowledging the rule of law and order, he does not stop to consider the consequences of his actions. He is essentially a loner with no loyalties or allegiances, and although his lack of anxiety and guilty feelings will deflect suspicion, he ultimately ceases to worry about protecting his interests and lays himself open to incrimination. However, murders committed by sexual psychopaths are among the most difficult to trace back to their perpetrators. The predictability and patterns which often emerge with motive in other crimes are missing here. Sex killers are totally unpredictable, with the knack of conducting themselves without creating the least suspicion. They are often cloaked with protective cunning, sufficiently aware that they have offended against society to exhibit intelligence and cool-headedness in covering up their tracks. Completely lacking emotion and devoid of guilt, they can commit the most terrible acts of violence and return home physically spent to fall into a deep sleep.

The hallmark of the sexual psychopath is writ large throughout the Babes in the Wood murders. Sexual gratification was the motive, sexual assault the intent. The *modus operandi* was the usual one of using charm or familiarity to lure victims to a lonely spot where, shrouded in privacy, he carried out his carnal exploitation. But this murderer, unlike Neville Heath or Peter Sutcliffe, was not dealing with adults with the intellectual and physical potential to resist him, but with two immature schoolchildren. Such was the nature of this beast. A truly evil man. This killer, like others of his type, probably lived under the cloak of urban respectability, possibly with a wife and children who were totally unsuspecting of his real nature.

Bishop certainly would have drawn attention to himself by wandering around the Wild Park area if he had had preconceived ideas about a sexual assault. Was he endowed with protective cunning? Ambling along Lewes Road in full sight of hundreds of travellers would seem stupid if he had just killed the girls. But could that not be interpreted as protective cunning? Was he cool-headed enough to cover his tracks? He wasn't being cool-headed when he lied about the newspaper and an attempt to steal a car, nor was there anything cool-headed about saying he had seen blood-flecked foam on Nicola's lips.

But Bishop was, as one observer cynically claimed, 'a sandwich short of a picnic', in other words, a bit dim. He liked to boast that the dog Misty was insured for thousands of pounds when it was not. Later, when he was in trouble as a suspect and being granted Legal Aid because he was penniless, he claimed he had hired a top

American lawyer. Ralph Haeems may be good but he is certainly not American.

So can a man sexually assault and murder two little girls then amble home along a busy road apparently without a care in the world? Arrive home, cook a meal, wash some clothes and enjoy a relaxing hot bath? Can that man, that murderer, turn up near the scene of the crime next day, gather up one of the dead girl's jumpers and help the poor mother search for a child he has recently killed? Again, we can turn to the case of Colin Pitchfork. During the evening of Monday, 21 November 1983 he drove his wife Carole to her evening class where she was studying to gain qualifications as a probation officer. He dropped her off at 7 p.m. Their baby was in a carrycot on the back seat of his Ford Escort. He collected his wife at 9 p.m. and murdered his first victim, Lynda Mann, in between. Carole did not suspect a thing.

So the answer is yes, Russell Bishop, if he *were* a sexual psychopath, could quite easily have conducted himself in the manner that he did. Those who know Bishop might say that he is a happy-go-lucky young man with not a bad thought in his head. There again, those who knew Pitchfork would say the same thing. Bishop, Pitchfork and John Cannan had reputations among their friends and workmates as insatiable womanisers. All three were also petty crooks.

Method is the third element involved in circumstantial evidence, which in this case is linked to the question of whether or not the girls knew their killer.

The prosecution maintained that one man, namely Russell Bishop, had murdered the girls in or very close to the children's den. The defence, on the other hand, took the view that the children had been killed elsewhere and were then moved to the den.

In the absence of any evidence that the girls had screamed, shouted for help, or had been spotted struggling with a person in the Wild Park, it may be reasonably assumed that they went to the den quite freely and of their own accord. While a scenario suggesting that the two girls were killed by a complete stranger who had followed them into the den, or happened upon them there, cannot be discounted entirely, it seems more likely that they either walked there with someone they knew very well indeed, or were seen entering the general area of the den by that someone.

But would the girls have gone into the den on their own so late in the evening? Karen knew that her mother had cooked her evening meal and that it was waiting for her at home, we know that Karen was reluctant to enter the park, so as far as Karen is concerned, the answer must be no. She would be in trouble enough for being late for her meal. We know from the evidence of several people and from the results of the post-mortem examination that Nicola had eaten some chips before her death; this was her dinner that evening. She *was* very keen to go into the park, but neither child would have gone into the park with a stranger at that hour.

The defence put forward the theory that the girls were murdered elsewhere, then moved later to the den, but there are crucial weaknesses to this argument. Examination of the scenes of crime photographs taken by Baynes shows that Nicola's feet are in deep undergrowth, just to the left of the opening of the den. If concealment had been a prime requisite in the killer's mind, he would have dragged the children's bodies further into the den and hidden them in the undergrowth. This was clearly not the case, for the girls were visible within fifteen feet of the den. The wooded area to the north of the Wild Park is extremely dense and runs up a steep incline to houses in Highlands and Coldean. The children's den was set deep in this wooded strip, so anywhere along that strip of dense undergrowth would have provided exactly the same degree of concealment. It does not make sense to imagine the girls being killed elsewhere, then lifted or dragged through that dense area or across to the den where they were found.

Whoever killed the girls knew about that children's den, of that there can be no doubt, which precludes a stranger as the murderer. The scenes of crime and forensic evidence illustrates how the children met their deaths. Arriving at the den in innocence with the killer, it may be imagined that initially the three just sat and talked. The man was overwhelmed by sexual desire. Emotions he could not control were exploding inside him. First he touched Nicola, perhaps softly to begin with, judging her reaction. Karen backed away, just a foot or so, sensing danger. Then, firmly, he took hold of Nicola and forced her down. She might have cried out to Karen, showing the first signs of panic. It was now dark and her mother would be annoyed. What had started as a bit of a lark with her friend was getting out of control. The man forced his hands inside Nicola's skirt; her clothes were becoming soiled with dirt. She screamed for help, then he hit her a powerful blow across the face, knocking her unconscious. Karen started to get up, to run, but there was nowhere to go. A strong hand grabbed her by the sweatshirt from behind, dragging her backwards into the den. Her knickers were wrenched off. The hand tightened around her neck, throttling her to death.

The killer then turned his hand to Nicola, oblivious of her friend's fate. He murdered Nicola where she lay, then sexually assaulted her again from behind after death. He next lifted Karen into his arms and placed her further into the cave over Nicky. At some later time during the night he discarded his 'Pinto' sweatshirt alongside the railway track near Moulsecoomb railway station.

9. Committed to Trial, Committed to Earth

Bishop's days of freedom were fast running out. He was due to answer to his bail on 4 December 1986 but was invited to return to John Street police station a day earlier. He arrived there at 10 a.m. on 3 December accompanied by his solicitor, Ralph Haeems. Detective Sergeant Swan and Detective Constable Wilkinson took him into an interview room and Wilkinson then said, 'I'm arresting you for the murders of Nicola Fellows and Karen Hadaway.' Bishop replied, after being cautioned, 'I'm not guilty, leave it out.' He was then formally charged with the double murder.

The following day, dressed in grey cord trousers, a powder blue zip-up jacket and black shoes, he arrived at Hove Magistrate's Court at 8.30 a.m., handcuffed to a police officer; outside the building a crowd had gathered in the drizzling rain. The charges having been read out to him, Bishop appeared before the Bench at 10 a.m. The families of the victims stayed away from the hearing, but two of Bishop's brothers sat in the public gallery and heard brief details of the case outlined by prosecutor Mr Geoffrey Clinton. A bespectacled Clerk of the Court read out the charges as Bishop stood ashen-faced in the dock, flanked by uniformed police officers.

Clinton said, 'On or about 9 October 1986 in the county of Sussex, Russell Bishop murdered Nicola Elizabeth Fellows and Karen Jane Michelle Hadaway.' Ralph Haeems said there would be no application for bail but, 'My client strenuously denies the offences.' Haeems asked the court to expedite the preparation of the papers connected with the case because of the nature of the charges and the fact that Bishop strongly denied them. There was no application for reporting restrictions to be lifted. Legal Aid was granted by the chairman of the Bench, Mr Reginald Fitch.

Bishop was remanded in custody for a week, but he would not be required to attend court again in person until 31 December. He left for Brixton Prison in a dark Bedford van.

Christmas was only nine cold days away. Weeping families and friends gathered at the Wild Park for a service of remembrance for Karen and Nicola. At a spot just yards away from where the nine-year-olds had died, two newly planted trees were blessed in their memory. Close by, a new bench had been placed bearing a plaque carrying the girls' names and referring to their tragic deaths. On the bench were floral tributes, including one depicting a Santa Claus holding a red rose and surrounded by Christmas tinsel.

The families were wrapped up in heavy coats to protect them from a bitter wind that whistled across the park. They listened with tears in their eyes as Father Marcus Ronchetti, priest in charge at the nearby St Mary Magdelan Church in Coldean, led the gathering in singing Psalm 23, 'The Lord is my Shepherd'. He spoke of the two new trees symbolising death in winter, and hope then life in summer. As people prepared for Christmas and the hope of the coming of Christ, he described the innocent girls as already being with the glory of God. Jonathan Fellows and Darren Hadaway wept; Barrie Fellows described the ceremony as 'marvellous and moving. The trees will be nice when they come into bloom – I thank the people of Moulsecoomb from the bottom of my heart.'

More than £7000 had been collected by the people of Brighton, of which £2500 had been set aside for the memorials and other expenses, including a headstone. Another £1000 would go to the local Youth Club, and £500 had been allocated to the grieving Hadaway and Fellows families to help with their expenses. The remainder had gone towards a £3000 blood and oxygen monitoring machine for the Royal Alexandra Hospital for Sick Children in Brighton. The families had received over a hundred cards and letters, some from prisoners at Lewes. Inmates at Ford Open Prison near Arundel raised £160. 'It is a noble effort when you think they only earn between £2.50 and £3.00 a week,' claimed Mr Eddie Parkinson, the Deputy Governor. 'It was a spontaneous gesture by the prisoners and shows their repugnance of the murders.'

Christmas came and went. Bishop was returned to Hove Magistrate's Court on the last day of the month. He declared his innocence three times. As the charges were read again to him, he shouted: 'May I correct you, sir, I didn't murder them girls . . .' Later in the hearing, almost in tears, Bishop interrupted his solicitor: 'I am innocent of all charges against me.' At the end of the hearing, as Bishop turned to leave the court escorted by two police officers, the chairman of the Bench said one of the reasons for objecting to further bail was the danger that Bishop would interfere with witnesses. Bishop turned and shouted, 'One thing is – there ain't no witnesses.' But then, how was he to know that?'

Haeems complained bitterly against the refusal of bail and the reason given for it, arguing that Bishop had received dozens of letters of support. 'It's all very well saying he will commit further offences, but I would like to see evidence of that. All that has been heard is rumour and innuendo.' But Bishop was remanded in custody at Brixton for another week. In the meantime, the coroner decided to release the girls' bodies for burial.

On Boxing Day, Bishop became a father again when Jennie gave birth to a daughter, whom they named Hayley. Sylvia Bishop, Russell's mother, was living through the worst days of her life. Convinced of her son's innocence, she visited him every day at Brixton, concerned about his welfare and his state of mind. When time would allow, she interviewed dozens of people in an effort to clear her son's name. Her problems were exacerbated by a series of desperate telephone calls from a young girl who claimed she had new evidence which was vital to Russell and his solicitors. She had rung the police, then Ralph Haeems. In tears, she explained to him that she had been threatened by someone with a beating if she ever telephoned anyone again. Brighton detectives then received a letter written in pencil, apparently in the hand of a young girl; wrapped in clingfilm, it was pushed through the mail slot of Moulsecoomb police box. The note claimed that the writer was terrified because she had been threatened by her boyfriend and an older boy who was a boxer. She also claimed she could not 'grass' on people because where she lived was a rough and tough area. Investigation brought to light a lonely woman, known as Christine, who was seeking attention; she was mentally sub-normal.

Karen and Nicola were buried at Bear Road Cemetery on 4 February 1987. Outside Nicola's house in the front garden was a row of large floral displays, including a Cabbage Patch Doll complete with a little girl's dress and a heart in yellow flowers. As relatives arrived, Mrs Hadaway wept outside her home and had to be comforted by her family. The fifteen-vehicle cortège was late leaving Newick Road; dozens of neighbours, many of them weeping, watched it pass. Beside the name of Nicky, picked out in pink on the roof of the hearse, was a message from Nicola's parents: 'For Nicky, our very precious daughter. Jesus has you in his care. We have you in our hearts. We will love and miss you always. Sleep well, little one.' Another from Nicky's fifteen-year-old brother Jonathan said: 'To my darling sister. I love and miss you very much. Be good with Jesus. Love from Jon.'

Mourners, young and old, wept during the 40-minute service. Thirty-year-old Father Ronchetti spoke to the grief-stricken parents: 'They were not by any stretch of the imagination angels. However, their young innocent lives were not corrupted by the wicked thoughts of this world.'

The girls were buried in white coffins next to each other in a double grave in the Children's Cemetery. The assembly of over a hundred grieving relatives and friends was barely visible through the eerie mist, but their cries of sorrow were all too clear.

Karen's mother had to be supported through the committal service. She wept in the arms of Wendy King, the WPC who had befriended the family soon after the deaths. Nicola's mother broke down after the service, crying out, 'Oh my baby, oh my baby.' Relatives held her, telling her to 'Let it go, let it all out.' Both fathers and several relatives wept uncontrollably as Father Ronchetti asked holy angels to lead the girls to eternal peace.

Two single roses were laid by the graves with the messages 'My love goes with you for ever and ever' and 'You have only gone to play. God bless you.' There was anger in the face of Barrie Fellows as the service ended. Friends held him as he, in turn, comforted his wife. The gathering slowly broke up as people walked in procession along the line of floral tributes, stopping occasionally to read the messages of sympathy. A few returned to the graves and stared down at the coffins; a heart-shaped cushion rested on Nicola's. A lone woman in black stood and cried until her husband led her away.

Police were on duty a discreet distance away, but apart from controlling traffic they had little else to do but watch the proceedings. After most of the mourners had drifted away, a young blonde-haired woman knelt between the two graves, her head bowed in prayer. She was led away in tears by her mother as pressmen approached. Four rows containing 130 wreaths and bouquets were laid out by the undertakers in the wet grass. At the heart of two separate displays were the names 'Karen' written in red carnations and 'Nicky' worded in pink, sent by the parents of each girl. The message to Karen read: 'Remembering a wonderful daughter. Now and forever in our hearts. You will always be loved and you will never be forgotten. Your loving mum and dad.'

Other tributes ranged from simple posies to teddy bears made of flowers. Among them were wreaths from the Sussex police and the inmates of Lewes Prison, the staff and pupils of Moulsecoomb Infant and Coldean Junior Schools, the Moulsecoomb Social Services office, the Hiker's Rest pub, the Coldean fish and chip shop, Mercury Cabs and Sussex singer Johnny Wakefield. That evening the families spent a few hours at the Hiker's Rest; it was the only place they could go. As the funeral had been in progress, at the precise moment when mourners broke into their final hymn in tremulous voice, 'All Things

Bright and Beautiful', a cruel thief had stolen a £15 pub collection towards the funeral expenses from the Bevendean Hotel in Hillside.

At HM Prison Brixton, Bishop was existing on food brought in by his mother and Jennie Johnson, such was his fear of being killed by shards of glass placed in his prison diet. His suspicions proved justified, for glass was found in his mashed potatoes. He looked pale and ill at the visits while on remand. He had reason to feel insecure, for he had already been branded a child killer by the prison population: the lowest form of prison life. Stripped of what little dignity remained to him, he claimed that the inhumane atmosphere was unbelievable. 'I remember going to meals and seeing broken glass glinting in the mash we were supposed to eat. I never had a proper meal all the time I was inside; only a few chips at the most. I had to live on fruit, biscuits and the crisps my family brought in.' The kitchen inmates spat in his food as it was passed through the serving hatch, salt was dumped in his tea, custard slopped into his gravy. More than once he 'slipped' down the stairs. He later claimed in the press that he was terrorised by prison staff who threatened him with horrifying injuries. Any complaint he made fell on deaf ears, but he soon requested the Govenor to place him in protective custody (Rule 43). His charges had been read by inmates who worked in the prison reception area, and before his admission had been fully documented the news spread like wildfire throughout Brixton, one of the toughest and most overcrowded jails in Britain.

'As soon as I'd appeared in court, a big police convoy took me to Brixton jail and I was rushed into the Hospital's F Wing. That's where the nutty prisoners go, to put it bluntly. After a week or two I was thwacked around the face with a bit of wood by another prisoner. He never said anything. Just hit me because of the crimes I was accused of. The pain soon went away, but there were constant threats against me. I was called a "nonce" – jail slang for a child-sex-beast. Other prisoners kicked their doors to try to frighten me and I could hear some of them screaming. One threw a cupful of scalding water at me one evening after we had slopped out. But it missed, thank God.

'I got a beating in April [1987] when I answered back to a warder. He just smacked me in the mouth. I had a fat lip but I wasn't badly hurt. I was even made to slop out at the double.' But his lowest ebb had come at Christmas 1986, 'not because everybody outside was enjoying themselves but because my girlfriend, Jennie, was having our second baby, Hayley.' Bishop tried to cope with the anguish by blocking reality from his mind. 'I just didn't want to know that she was having our child. I tried to shut it out.'

While he was in prison the police work ground on to bring a case against him at trial, and equal efforts were made to establish a defence. There was a long time to wait.

10. Evidence and Questions: 1

The case against Russell Bishop was going to rest primarily on forensic evidence, resulting from tests made on trace elements found on or near the bodies and on items belonging to or connected with Bishop. Apart from tests to establish the presence of car-spraying compounds on Bishop's clothing and the 'Pinto' sweatshirt, there were others involving a variety of fibres and hairs.

The examination of human hairs is an important aspect of crime investigation for the potential it offers to relate a suspect or a victim to a crime scene – part of the chain of evidence whereby hairs and fibres are transferred as a result of contact between assailant and victim.

Viewed longitudinally, human hair can be seen to consist of three parts. The sheath has a characteristic combination of scale-shape and pattern; several schemes exist for the classification of these patterns into a number of basic types. Human hairs have a rather faint surface-scale pattern, of which an impression can be made if necessary. The cortex is the substance of the hair and normally contains any pigment present. Finally, there is the medulla, a central core which contains air; it can be continuous and uniform, irregularly interrupted or totally absent, and its diameter relative to that of the whole hair is variable. The appearance of hair in cross-section is also an identifying characteristic and there are various techniques for cutting and examining cross-hair sections. A hair can also be characterised to some extent by its colour and general appearance, but these can never tie it to a particular individual.

Head hairs are smooth and regular, circular in cross-section if straight, elliptical if curly. Recent cutting, singeing, bleaching, dyeing and the old-fashioned methods of permanent waving all produce characteristic recognisable alterations. Hair which has been lacquered shows distinctive adherent blobs of dried lacquer. Beard and moustache hairs, as well as being fairly thick, are occasionally roughly triangular in cross-section. Eyebrows hairs and eyelashes have long, fine, tapering tips. (More than one assailant who has kicked his victim in the face has been convicted by eyebrow hairs wedged into the toe of his shoe.) Body hairs (pubic and axillar) are, as well as being short, coarse and curly, nearly always elliptical in cross-section and usually medullated. The comparison of pubic hairs is, of course, important in the investigation of many sexual offences. Any good optical microscope is adequate for hair examination, but some features, especially the surface scales and dried lacquer blobs, are more clearly revealed by the scanning electron microscope.

The characterisation of hair by means of the trace elements it contains has attracted considerable interest in recent years. This obviously requires an exceedingly sensitive method of analysis and, during the last decade, research in several countries, particularly Canada, Belgium and Great Britain, has led to the use of neutron activation analysis for this purpose. Radio-chemical analysis was used in France during the 1950s in connection with the notorious Besnard arsenic poisoning case and is still the best known and most widely used application of radioactivity in forensic science. The sample is irradiated with a high neutron flux to convert the elements into their radioactive isotopes; these are then identified by the characteristic energies and rates of decay (inversely proportional to the half lives) of the radiation emitted. Neutron activation analysis was used as part of the investigation of the Michigan Murders in 1970 and helped secure the conviction of Norman Collins for seven murders.

Without doubt, neutron analysis is one of the most sensitive methods yet devised, enabling very small amounts of trace elements to be determined. However, it is probably fair to say that it has not been proved an indispensable tool to the forensic scientist, as seemed likely when it was first introduced into the field. An atomic reactor is needed to provide this neutron flux, which obviously limits the use of the method to laboratories having access to one. It is relatively time-consuming, the equipment is costly and a very high degree of specialised expertise is necessary if the results are to be accurate and reliable. The method is more commonly used in Canada and the USA than in Britain. Early results, particularly those reported from Canada by Dr J. Jervis, led to an over-optimistic belief that it was possible to 'tie' a hair conclusively to the head from which it came. Later researches, notably those carried out in Belgium and also in Britain by the Atomic Weapons Research Establishment on behalf of the Home Office, have tended to confirm a more cautious approach. Nevertheless, Aldermaston had this facility and one wonders why, in view of the general expense of the Wild Park investigation, this technique was not employed in this case.

The present position may be briefly summarised as follows.

Hair contains a variety of trace elements including zinc, gold, copper, manganese, arsenic, chlorine and bromine. These elements are derived mainly from the diet but also to some extent by applications, such as shampoo and conditioners. It is not technically difficult to determine the concentrations of those elements in quite small samples of hair. These concentrations vary between one person and another and also, to a lesser degree, between different parts of the same head. Some elements show a much greater range of concentration than others. They may also change with time in one individual. The hair of persons sharing the same diet and environment tends to show less variation than that of the population at large.

Two specimens of hair from the same head taken at about the same time are likely to resemble each other in general composition more than either resembles a random specimen from another head. The differences in the latter case may range from negligible to very great, depending on the elements considered. Knowledge of the distributions of all these elements in a large population makes it possible to calculate mathematically the probability that two specimens of hair did not come from the same head if the concentrations of trace elements in them differ by more than an accepted amount. A statistical procedure designed to deal with this aspect has been developed by J. B. Parker of the Atomic Weapons Research Establishment.

A high-power microscope is the initial means of identifying and comparing recovered fibres. Wool and cotton fibres, as well as most other natural fibres, exhibit a characteristic microscopic structure, and rarely is any other identification technique necessary. But many man-made fibres present more difficult problems, and other techniques are brought into use, for example chemical solvent tests, bi-refringence determinations and infra-red spectrometry.

Bi-refringence is an optical property of most fibres and depends upon the way in which light passing through the fibre is slowed down differentially. Polarised light – light which vibrates in only one plane – emerges as two components when passed through a fibre. In one, the light vibrates parallel to the length of the fibre, and in the other, the light vibrates at right angles to the length of the fibre and is therefore out of phase on emergence. Thus the fibre has two refractive indices and the difference between the refractive index of the fibre in one direction and that in the other is termed the bi-refringence value. These values are different for different types of fibre and they are useful diagnostic features.

Spectrometry in the visible and ultraviolet regions of the spectrum are used in both drug analysis and in the analysis of fibre dyestuffs. In the latter, the amount of dyestuff in the fibre fragment is very small and the method of analysis of visible spectrometry has been miniaturised, using an instrument called a microspectro-photometer attached to a microscope.

Once the fibre type has been identified, the scientist can proceed to compare it with fibres from a known source. Optical microscopy, using a comparison microscope fitted with white, blue-fluorescent and ultraviolet sources, is employed here. Diameter, cross-sectional shape, longi-tudinal striations and other internal features, as well as fibre colour, are compared by this means.

The principle that matter can be transferred from one object to another is central to forensic scientific examin-ation. In the case of transfer of fibres, there have been two specific studies to establish the factors which cause transference and which affect the number of fibres exchanged. The dominant means of transfer were shown to be:

i.   shedding of loose fibres
ii. disentanglement of whole fibres in the body of the yarn
iii. fracturing of a whole fibre and release of the fragments

Despite having superficially smooth surfaces, all fabrics will, to some extent, lose fibres by one or more of the above means. The numbers of fibres, however, was found to vary according to:

i.   the nature of the recipient fabric; whether it was rough or fine in texture
ii. the fibre composition of a recipient fabric
iii. the nature of the donor fabric, which influences the numbers of fibres transferred
iv. contact pressure up to a maximum level, after which increasing pressure does not cause more fibres to be released and transferred

The fabrics from which cloths, carpets and soft furnishings are made are woven from different types and colours of yarn. The yarns used in weaving processes are made from naturally occurring fibres such as wool, cotton and linen, or man-made fibres such as nylon, rayon, acrylic and polyester. All these fibre types can be dyed to produce a variety of colours as required. It is a feature of many cloths that they shed tiny fragments of fibres. These fragments rest on the surface of the cloth and remain there until they are either brushed off or transferred to another cloth with which they come into contact.

It is normal laboratory practice to remove hairs and fibres from clothing by pressing strips of adhesive tape similar to Sellotape on to garments. The sections of tape are then stuck on to sheets of clear plastic and examined under a microscope; selected hairs or fibres are removed and mounted on microscopic slides for closer scrutiny. Having examined both tapings and slides, fibres or hairs are taken selectively in order to prove the connection which is wanted by the prosecution.

Regina *v.* Russell Bishop was listed at the Lewes Crown Court for 10 a.m., 23 November 1987. The trial judge was to be Mr Justice Schiemann, presiding over his first murder trial. Mr Brian Leary QC and Mr R. Owen appeared on behalf of the prosecution, Mr Ivan Lawrence QC, MP, and Mr C. Conway appearing for the defence. Lawrence had been defence counsel for Denis Nilsen, the killer of at least fifteen homosexuals and vagrants, at his Old Bailey trial in 1983.

For several days the court listened to the evidence against Bishop. It was then the turn of Dr Anthony Peabody, the prosecution's main witness, to give his evidence. The case rested on the prosecution's ability to prove links between the clothing worn by himself and the two girls, to establish that they had been in contact. Dr Peabody was one of the senior staff at the Home Office Forensic Science Laboratory at Aldermaston. Forensic defence was conducted by Independent Scientific and Investigation Services, run by Ruth and B. F. Callan.

Central to the issue was the examination of the 'Pinto' sweatshirt which the police were convinced the killer had worn; they were equally convinced that it belonged to Russell Bishop. The hair and fibre tests on it were crucial to their case. Apart from items already mentioned as retrieved from the den in the Wild Park, scenes of crime officers had collected six more items there on Sunday, 12 October 1986, labelled EWR/30 to EWR/35; among

them were controlled soil samples and a fibre from one of
their own white anti-contamination suits for comparison
tests. Redman had already collected two blue fibres from
the death scene: EWR/16, found on a path, and
EWR/29, found on the ground near the den entrance,
along with twelve more items including a piece of wood,
more fibres and a jam jar which had become entangled in
undergrowth at the base of a tree. Dr Peabody himself had
searched for clues with Redman, finding eleven items
which he labelled AJP/1 to AJP/11.

Dr Peabody had examined the blue 'Pinto' sweatshirt
(DE/1): it was a mid-blue sweatshirt with long sleeves
and a round neck, and a white printed motif with the
name 'Pinto' on the left breast. It was well worn, in poor
condition and, judging from the stench of body odour,
had not recently been washed. There was a very small
amount of human blood on the back of the right cuff, but
insufficient for grouping purposes. Fibres and debris had
been removed from the garment for further examination.
On the light blue-grey trousers taken from Bishop's house
he found no blood but did locate several areas of paint-like
staining, particularly on the seat, thighs and left calf.
Fibres had been removed for further examination from
Marion Stevenson's greenish-turquoise jumper and skirt.
It is of interest to note that the 40-inch chest 'Pinto' would
have been several sizes too large for Bishop. The police
never asked him to try on the garment and they were
aware that Bishop, who had a 34-inch chest, liked to wear
all his sweatshirts and jumpers skin-tight.

It is not in dispute that the 'Pinto' sweatshirt and the
tops worn by the two girls were in contact. Karen always
wore her green school uniform to school; when she came
home she changed into more casual wear to go out and
play. No child would be allowed out to rough and tumble

in the clothing that had to be kept smart for school, and from talks with the Hadaways I am convinced that this change of clothes was the general rule. The evening of 9 October 1986 was the one exception. Karen came home and was allowed out to play for a short while. The intention of her mother was that she would pop up to their local shop, H. A. Wrights in Coldean Lane, come home, eat her supper, collect her younger sister from a neighbour and then change her school uniform before going out with her mother to visit a family friend. Nicola did not possess a school uniform and consequently wore an assortment of jumpers and sweatshirts to school. On 9 October 1986 she had chosen a pink sweatshirt. It could have been blue, green or yellow. Therefore the combination of green and pink tops worn by the two girls out of school hours must suggest that contact between the three garments – the two coloured tops worn by the girls and the blue 'Pinto' – could have only happened on that day and on no other.

From past experience, Peabody knew that the blue 'Pinto' fibres were acrylic and that the green and pink fibres were polyester. Results of a survey had told him that acrylic fibres were frequently used for jumpers and warm upper garments but seldom for any other items, such as skirts or trousers. Polyester fibres are used in a wider range of clothing, predominantly jackets, jumpers, shirts and trousers. The particular colours, pink and green in this case, indicated less likelihood that the fibres were from trousers, while their thickness indicated that they were not from a shirting fabric. Therefore he had very good reason to form the professional opinion that the fibres from each parent garment were indeed from that garment.

He then began to cross-check each garment for con-tamination fibre transference. In this he came up trumps.

There were eleven green and four pink polyester fibres on the 'Pinto', microscopically indistinguishable from the polyester fibres of which Karen's and Nicola's upper garments were made. There were nine blue acrylic fibres on the pink sweatshirt labelled 'Fellows' and eleven blue acrylic fibres on the green sweatshirt labelled 'Hadaway'. These blue fibres were microscopically indistinguishable from the blue materials of which the 'Pinto' was made. Single blue fibres from the 'Pinto' were also found on the taping taken from the back of Karen's T-shirt (IEW/2) and from the left-hand side of Karen's skirt (IEW/9).

Further, there were four blue acrylic fibres on the blue-grey trousers (JNJ/1) which matched in every respect those that made up the 'Pinto'. There were also five turquoise-green polyester fibres on the 'Pinto' that had come from the towelling top and skirt belonging to Marion Stevenson. Peabody concluded that here was a definite and conclusive link between the dead children, Russell Bishop and Marion Stevenson – the first primary link between the 'Pinto', Bishop and murder.

However, Peabody did not find any cross-contamination of matching fibres from the two girls' sweatshirts to the blue-grey trousers, nor any fibres from the trousers on either of the girls' sweatshirts. Why, one might ask, if there were green and pink fibres on the 'Pinto' and 'Pinto' fibres on the trousers – and it was alleged that Bishop wore the 'Pinto' at the time of the killings – why are there no green and pink fibres on the trousers? The reason why no matching fibres were found on Bishop's trousers, if there were any to be found, was simply that Dr Peabody did not examine them for the purpose of finding pink and green fibres. When asked in court why he had not conducted this very elementary examination, he replied with words to the effect that he had not been asked to. As Bishop never denied that the trousers were his nor that he had worn them on 9 October, this test could have been important in establishing his direct guilt of the crime, or lack of it. But what of the four blue fibres from the 'Pinto' that had become attached to the trousers and how did they get there if the 'Pinto' did not belong to him or if he had not been wearing it? The answer seemed simple enough to the defence: both garments, it was alleged, were thrown together at Brighton police station before being bagged up for transport to Aldermaston for tests.

Lawrence, for the defence, wanted to know whether Peabody was saying that the 'Pinto' was worn by Bishop or by the murderer, as these extracts from the trial transcript show:

Lawrence: 'Let me just ask you that again. Using your scientific powers of analysis, for which purpose you have been asked to give evidence in this case, you are not saying to the jury scientifically that the "Pinto" sweatshirt was worn by the murderer?'
Peabody: 'No, I am not.'
Lawrence: 'All you are saying is that it could have been?'
Peabody: 'Yes.'

Doubt had been injected.

Lawrence: 'The second thing is this: using all the scientific expertise, you are not saying that that "Pinto" was ever worn by Bishop?'
Peabody: 'No, I am not saying that either.'
Lawrence: 'All you are saying is that it could have been?'
Peabody: 'Yes.'

The chief prosecution witness had just confirmed to the jury that Bishop may or may not have ever worn the

'Pinto', which was the only worthwhile piece of police evidence against him.

Lawrence: 'Thank you. Now let us just see why it is you are saying these things, because I am reluctant to just sit down and leave it, for a number of reasons which will become obvious. Your evidence, though doubtless accurate as to what you found, is highly selective, is it not?'
Peabody: 'In what way?'
Lawrence: 'Did the police give you an outline of what their case was against Bishop?'
Peabody: 'I am aware of the broad outlines of the case. I cannot say really that I have ever been a party in any great detail to what the police have been doing as a result of this case.'
Lawrence: 'Were you ever asked to see if you could find anything which linked the "Pinto" to the murder?'

Peabody seemed to be wary of the question or did not understand it.

Peabody: 'To what?'
Lawrence: 'To the murder, the killing of the two little girls?'
Peabody: 'Yes.'
Lawrence: 'Were you ever asked if you could find any evidence to link the "Pinto" to Douggie Judd?'
Peabody: 'I do not know who Douggie Judd is.'
Lawrence: 'So we can say no?'
Peabody: 'No.'
Lawrence: 'To Barrie Fellows?'
Peabody: 'No.'
Lawrence: 'To Marion Stevenson?'
Peabody: 'Marion Stevenson, yes, Marion Stevenson, we have her clothing.'

Lawrence: 'But the purpose of examining the one item of her clothing, her suit top and bottom – you only ever examined the suit of Marion Stevenson, did you not?'

Peabody: 'Yes, I did.'

Lawrence: 'The purpose was not to see if she was linked to the murder, but to see if Bishop was linked to the murder?'

Peabody: 'No, the reason for the examination was to identify to whom the "Pinto" might belong.'

Lawrence: 'Your brief was to find if you could – I am not suggesting you were asked to find it at all costs – anything which showed that the "Pinto" had been worn by Bishop?'

Peabody: 'Yes.'

Lawrence: 'And that is the significance of Marion Stevenson's suit?'

Peabody: 'Quite so.'

Lawrence: 'If you had been asked to find out whether Marion Stevenson had been linked to the murders you would have been given a whole lot more of her clothing, would you?'

Peabody: 'Presumably so, yes.'

Lawrence: 'So that is what I mean by being selective. The job or exercise, if you could accomplish it, was to see what links there were between Bishop and the "Pinto", not what links there were between anybody else and the "Pinto"?'

Peabody: 'Yes.'

Having done much to establish doubt as to whether Bishop owned or wore the 'Pinto' and whether police enquiries into it had been one-sided, Lawrence then went on to question Peabody about the source of the green fibres from Karen's school top and perhaps indirectly suggesting that there might have been some mistake or confusion over the fibres used in evidence.

The Aldermaston laboratory contained 5339 items which might shed fibre but, according to Peabody, the green polyester fibres of Karen's sweatshirt had no match among them, which led him to the conclusion that these were uncommon fibres. On this point Lawrence and Peabody wrangled for some time, even the judge involving himself in the question in an attempt to make clear what was being said and, no doubt, to establish its significance to the jury. At last Peabody exclaimed:

'You do not understand what I am saying; you are mistaking the fact that Coldean School has green acrylic jumpers. They may well have had green jumpers for years and years and years, and they may all look alike to you. To me they look different, and this one to which we are referring is uncommon. The next Coldean School jumper you see will be slightly different; to an untutored eye it may just be an ordinary green polyester jumper which may be worn by all of Coldean School, but this is *not the case.*'

Lawrence: 'Were there any other fibres on the green sweatshirt?'
Peabody: 'Yes.'
Lawrence: 'There were. How many?'
Peabody: 'Hundreds.'
Lawrence: 'Did you match any of those with clothing from Barrie Fellows, Douggie Judd, Marion Stevenson, Jennie Johnson, Kevin Rowland, Marchant or any other suspect?'

Mr Leary for the Crown rocketed to his feet with an objection:

'Again my learned friend must be careful. He has just

used the words "or any other suspect". Your lordship took issue at an earlier stage of this trial with the use of those words when my learned friend was cross-examining one of the first witnesses to be called.'

Mr Justice Schiemann: 'I would have been happier if he had said: "Any other person involved with this case who might conceivably have had contact with the girls."'
Lawrence: 'I apologise. In the Magistrate's Court one officer did say that there were nine other suspects, and that is a point I would want to take up in due course.'

To maintain the thesis that Bishop did own the 'Pinto', it follows that at some time the garment must have been in his home and in contact with other items of his or Jennie Johnson's property. On Friday, 7 November 1986, Edward Redman and other officers had carried out a thorough examination of 17 Stephen's Road, taking a great many samples obtained by wiping adhesive tape across many items and articles of clothing. Apart from confiscating a pair of fingerless red rubber gloves from a larder cupboard, they took tapings from 25 items including underwear, the baby's clothing, sweatshirts and fluffy toys. These tapings were labelled EWR/83 to EWR/106. The officers examined the drain plug of Bishop's washing machine and again no matching blue fibres were discovered – the fact that the 'Pinto' had obviously not been recently washed may have had something to do with this.

During the research for this book, I wrote to Dr Peabody to ask if he or the laboratory might wish to contribute. Peabody telephoned me expressing a desire to help where he could, but on 15 May 1989 I received a formal open reply from Mr D. Neylan, director of the laboratory:

'Dear Mr Berry-Dee,

I have seen your letters to Dr Peabody, who is one of my senior staff and, in particular, the scientist who investigated the murder of Karen Hadaway and Nicola Fellows.

It is with regret that I must decline to allow Dr Peabody to assist you in your current project. The Hadaway-Fellows case has, as you know, been investigated, tried and brought to a current conclusion by the verdict of a jury. Dr Peabody's evidence in that case shows what it shows (and you may be assured that it was based on thorough work by one of the country's leading forensic scientists). Any further comment by Dr Peabody, either directly or by inference, would be inconsistent with the principles of the English Criminal Justice System.

I am fully aware that this case is of considerable interest and is likely to remain so, but I hope you will understand the stance I must take.

Yours sincerely,

D. Neylan (Director)'

When Callan and his wife Ruth wanted to conduct defence forensic tests at Aldermaston they found their work greatly hindered by red tape. Callan wrote to Ralph Haeems, Bishop's solicitor, on 8 October 1987:

'As you know, Ruth and I have been to Aldermaston three times so far. On the first day very little was done because little co-operation was given and indeed it was very much like a strict work-to-rule by both the laboratory and the police.

'To explain in detail, the police exhibits officer produced three exhibits for examination. When we asked for the others, we were told that they had not been asked for and were therefore not available. When we asked for a full list of exhibits in order that we could make application for specific items, this again was refused by the police. The result was that we could not order up specific exhibits and the police would not supply us with a list.'

Callan requested twenty days minimum to carry out the defence examinations of the exhibits. They were permitted only three days. Callan claimed that:

'. . . we were not prepared to take a fee for a perfunctory defence examination and . . . I saw no reason why, in the name of justice, we should not have the same number of man-hours available as the prosecution. This would substantially be reduced by close co-operation, therefore obviating repetition of scientific work – but this was not accepted.' Callan continued:

'The second and third visits, which were made following my conversation with yourself [Ralph Haeems], proved much better. While there was no co-operation which could have allowed areas of agreement, and therefore the saving of considerable time, there was at least no dragging of feet in supplying equipment, microscopes etc, and the atmosphere was more congenial. We did in fact receive a full list of exhibits – but not until the third and last day. We were not therefore able at that stage to look into the relationships between some items. We were obviously unaware of the course of the police investigation and hence their reasons why certain items were collected, but others [e.g. clothing from the persons (names removed from the text)] were not.'

Another point-blank refusal came when Callan requested to see the laboratory forms, which would have indicated to him the nature of the scientific work requested by the police. Callan was clearly irritated by the police refusal. He wrote:

'. . . It is crucial to understand the importance of these forms (which we were refused permission to see) because they can ask the scientist specifically to examine (for example) the blue "Pinto" sweatshirt for fibres from the pink and green sweatshirts, while ignoring virtually everything else. The scientist [Peabody], however, may jot down in his notes the presence of other debris. Some of this information may be of great evidential significance to the defence, although might not be mentioned in statements.'

In other words, had Peabody in fact discovered fibres that might have linked the 'Pinto' to another suspect or person, the defence would have been none the wiser. Callan went on to say:

'Despite much frustrated pushing on my part, the police would only say three things; viz:

i.   Your instructing solicitor has the information; get it from him.
ii. Tell me exactly the items you want and I will put in a request.
iii. That is not for me to answer.'

Number iii applied even when Callan asked for an indication of the defendant's height.

'Ruth was able to examine microscopic slides which had been made up by mounting various selected fibres from the three exhibits (the pink and green sweatshirts of the two girls, and the "Pinto" sweatshirt). This was allowed because they were part of the three exhibits. While she spent some time doing this, I tried to engage the two police representatives in "weather and flowers" conversation in order to stop Ruth feeling crowded in by the hovering attitude. A very difficult and off-putting thing to work with, as you will understand.'

Callan gives another graphic demonstration of the difficulties encountered by the forensic defence team with the

The Fibre Evidence

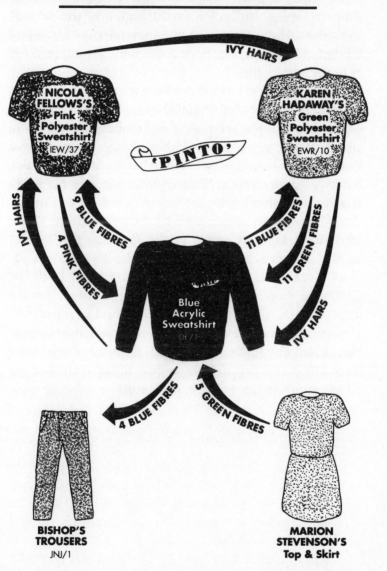

examination of fibres and hairs adhering to the tapings before their selective transference to slides.

'(a) There appears to be a fibre exchange between the children's pink and green sweatshirts and the "Pinto" sweatshirt. There are, however, other hairs and fibres and tapings, which is to be expected, but these are not referred to in the statements.

'(b) The suspect has a dog which we understand sheds hairs very easily. An examination of the defendant's clothing has shown a considerable number of hairs which, although not yet examined thoroughly by us, appear similar to dog hairs. It would seem that the fact that no dog hairs were found on the "Pinto" sweatshirt, while being in relative profusion on the defendant's clothing in general, should have been investigated by the Police/Home Office laboratory, as it all points to the fact that the "Pinto" sweatshirt may not have belonged to the defendant at all.'

As revealed in the cross-examination of Dr Peabody, Callan went on to point out that although fibres from the girls' sweatshirts and the 'Pinto' were found on other individuals' clothing, the examination of those garments was not carried any further. The fact that someone else could have killed the girls did not appear to have crossed the closed minds of the police investigators.

11. Evidence and Questions: 2

Apart from identification of fibres, the forensic tests concentrated on the presence on various items of clothing of hairs – human hairs, dog hairs and epidermal ivy hairs – and of red paint or compound.

The dog in question was Misty, taken by Bishop to help in the search for the two girls. Dr Peabody had already stated that although dog hairs had been found on other of Bishop's clothing, none had been found on the 'Pinto'. The police had taken samples directly from the dog, which was predominantly white with patches of brown and black, from which Peabody could work. In court he was questioned on his findings:

Leary: 'You have told us that Mrs Callan took some dog hairs from the sweatshirt, Court Exhibit 21 [Pinto], which did not come from Misty. Are there any other dog hairs on the "Pinto"?'
Peabody: 'There are. I removed three dog hairs from the sweatshirt, which I matched with the control sample from Misty.'

The judge intervened: 'So the position is that the ones that Mrs Callan removed from the sweatshirt did not match Misty's and the ones that you removed did?'

This rather contradicted both Peabody's and Callan's earlier report that they could find no dog hairs on the 'Pinto'.

On the issue of dog hairs, Lawrence almost over-stretched himself.

Lawrence: 'Did you see, did you notice there were dog hairs on the tapings from the "Pinto" other than those Mrs Callan asked you to take off? Did you notice there were others?'

Peabody: 'I did not examine them at the time. I examined them afterwards.'

Lawrence: 'It just so happened examining them afterwards, you happened to find three . . .?'

Peabody: 'The fact remains, I did.'

Lawrence: 'From Mr Russell Bishop's dog?'

Mr Justice Schiemann: 'Your phraseology "It just so happened . . .". Are you suggesting this witness tampered with the evidence?'

Lawrence: 'I make no suggestion, my lord. It is the interesting coincidence that he (a) never examined them before 29 October, (b) when Mrs Callan examined them, she did not notice them and, (c) when she examined them, he did not notice them and nothing was found until the next day. I do not make any conclusion from it. It is just coincidence.'

Mr Justice Schiemann: 'If you are not making any conclusions . . . I thought you were.'

Dr Peabody was furious.

Peabody: 'May I just make a note, please?'

Lawrence: 'What actually are you doing?'

Peabody: 'I am reminding myself about the possibility of tampering with clothing. I must remind myself this has been said.'

Lawrence: 'I am sorry, would you mind telling us . . .?'

Peabody: 'I shall remind myself later, if need be, that this allegation has at least been aired. I must say, I have not tampered with anything.'

Mr Justice Schiemann: 'It is something I said. You have written it down for what purpose?'
Peabody: 'That I can remember it has been said, for my own purpose.'

The argument went on for a few minutes, with Peabody ending: '. . . that the word "tampering" has been raised and I have not tampered with anything.'

In the end it was agreed that although dog hairs were found on the 'Pinto' they could not be assigned to Misty, though dog hairs on other of Bishop's clothing could. Apparently, identification of animal hairs is even more problematic than that of human hairs.

Dr Iain West, the Home Office pathologist, had discovered three human hairs and one fibre on the vulva of Nicola Fellows which were sent to Aldermaston for Dr Peabody's appraisal. He had samples of Bishop's head and body hairs for comparison.

Lawrence: 'Can you help us. Three hairs and one fibre were found by Dr West around Nicola's vulva?'
Peabody: 'Yes.'
Lawrence: 'Did you examine those?'
Peabody: 'No.'
Lawrence: 'Did somebody examine them?'
Peabody: 'No.'
Lawrence: 'The significance would be that somebody, if they had tried to have intercourse with Nicola, then their hairs might be what was found?'
Peabody: 'Might be.'

Lawrence took an incredulous air and looked at the jury. His voice raised an octave.

Lawrence: 'And are you saying nobody has examined them?'

Peabody: 'Nobody has examined them.'

Lawrence: 'At any rate, it is not part of your case that hairs found anywhere near Nicola's vulva could have come from Bishop. Bishop did give his pubic hairs for examination, did he not?'

Peabody: 'Yes, he did.'

Police officers sitting in court were seen to be holding their heads in their hands.

After a brief re-examination by Mr Leary for the Crown, Mr Justice Schiemann suggested that the hairs and the single fibre be examined. On 30 November Dr Peabody stepped once again into the witness box to give his evidence following the new tests.

Leary: 'Dr Peabody, when you were giving evidence previously before the court, you recall my lord suggested that you should examine one of the items which had been submitted to the laboratory, to see if you could find hairs in the item which had been submitted?'

The item was labelled IEW/55, a clear plastic envelope.

Peabody: 'Yes.'

Leary: 'I wonder if you would take, please, Exhibit 67, which is marked IEW/55. We have been told by Dr West, the pathologist, that he, using forceps, removed debris from the vicinity of the vulva of Nicola Fellows which was transferred into IEW/55, and in the exhibit label he has identified his signature as the first of three. He told us that the second signature appears to be that of the officer to whom it was handed in the laboratory?'

Peabody: 'Yes.'

Leary: 'And whose is the third signature?'

Peabody: 'Mine.'

Leary: 'Did you then receive that sealed item amongst a number of others on 13 October last year?'
Peabody: 'I did.'
Leary: 'And apart from bearing the identification mark IEW/55, how else is it described?'
Peabody: 'It is labelled "Debris around vulva (Fellows)".'
Leary: 'That is how we know it came from Nicola's vulva, apparently?'
Peabody: 'Yes.'
Leary: 'Was that item examined at the laboratory in connection with your investigation into this case?'
Peabody: 'It has been examined, yes.'
Leary: 'Well, at the time when you gave evidence here last, had it been examined then at the laboratory?'
Peabody: 'No.'
Leary: 'Did you examine it on 26 November of this year after you had completed giving your evidence and as a result of my lord's suggestion?'
Peabody: 'I have, yes.'
Leary: 'And what does that exhibit contain?'
Peabody: 'This exhibit contained a small, colourless wool fibre and a fibrous, hair-like piece of vegetation and there was also a small, pale mineral particle.'

Mr Lawrence took up the questioning.

Lawrence: 'You tell us, Dr Peabody, that you examined this exhibit and you found one small, colourless wool fibre?'
Peabody: 'Yes.'
Lawrence: 'And a fibrous, hair-like piece of vegetation?'
Peabody: 'Yes.'
Lawrence: 'And a small, pale mineral particle. What did that look like?'
Peabody: 'Just what it was – I do not know what it was – it

was hard and it looked like a mineral. It might be pale to a very pale, almost white.'

Lawrence: 'But what was it – a round thing?'

Peabody: 'No, it was angular. It was about one millimetre long by half a millimetre wide.'

Lawrence: 'So that cannot have been a hair?'

Peabody: 'Absolutely not. No.'

Lawrence: 'Well, what Dr West took, forcep by forcep, with great care, from the body – from Nicola's vulva – was three hairs or hair-like material and one fibre. He said in his statement: "three hairs and one piece of fibre".'

Mr Justice Schiemann: 'Can you give the reference?'

Lawrence: 'It is page eighty-six of his statement, my lord.' To the witness: 'What has happened to those four pieces?'

Peabody: 'Well, they are not there . . . When you say "What has happened to them?" I only found these two bits in here, but remembering that it is only a small plastic bag . . . It is quite possible for fibres to not be transferred properly even though you take great care. It is possible for them not actually to enter into the bag.'

Lawrence: 'What would you have put these three hairs and the fibre into, if not this plastic receptable?'

Peabody: 'I might have used a piece of Sellotape to stick the fibres on.'

Lawrence: 'So you would have kept the three hairs and one fibre if you had used Sellotape?'

Peabody: 'Yes.'

Lawrence: 'You run a distinct risk of losing something . . .?'

Peabody: 'It is a risk. It is very hard to make sure that fibres are transferred like this.'

Lawrence: 'It is careless, then, to put these three hairs and a fibre in a plastic receptacle where they might disappear?'

He might have added that it was equally careless to sign for such items without being sure that they were present.

Mr Lawrence then took up the clear plastic bag and, with squinting eyes, remarked, 'Well I cannot see anything.'

Peabody: 'Well, you will not, because they are in my bag.'
Lawrence: 'Oh, I see, they are not here – they are in your bag. Have they been in your bag all the morning?'
Peabody: 'Yes, they have.'
Lawrence: 'Have you taken them out of your bag at all?'
Peabody: 'Just now, yes.'
Lawrence: 'Not before this morning?'
Peabody: 'No.'
Lawrence: 'Because Dr West was asked to look at the hairs and he identified this as the hairs.'

Mr Leary leapt in.

'He identified it as hairs, Mr Lawrence, he identified the sealed package as being the package into which he had placed the debris and the exhibit label which he signed.'

Lawrence: 'I am sorry, I thought he was identifying the hairs as the ones he had examined. I am sorry if I made that mistake.'
Mr Justice Schiemann: 'Well, I made the same mistake. It just shows how one can jump to conclusions. My note is not clear.'

If the judge was confused, one might imagine that the jury hadn't a single idea what was going on.

Dr Peabody did not carry out any comparison tests on the head hairs given by Bishop for examination until the day after Ruth Callan came to Aldermaston and found human hairs on the 'Pinto'.

Lawrence: 'I notice from your diagram that you have on it eight head hairs marked "Bishop".'

Peabody: 'Correct.'

Lawrence: 'You are not saying that these eight head hairs certainly came from Bishop, are you?'

Peabody: 'No.'

Lawrence: 'Only that they could have come from Bishop?'

Peabody: 'They could have come from Bishop.'

Lawrence: 'But they might well have not done so?'

Peabody: 'They might not have.'

Mr Justice Schiemann interrupted: 'How many people in this country do you think have the same sort of hair structure, as far as analysis in hair is concerned, as of Mr Bishop. Are we talking about three, three thousand or three million?'

Peabody: 'I am afraid we don't know. All we are saying is that this head hair could have come from Russell Bishop, or hair like his. It would not have come from someone who had very dark or very pale hair.'

Lawrence: 'You have no idea to the crucial question of how common that hair is?'

Peabody: 'Absolutely none.'

Lawrence: 'Just so we can understand what you mean by that: not only do a lot of people have the same colour hair as Mr Bishop, but even the same person with the same head of hair has different sizes of hair?'

Peabody: 'Yes.'

Lawrence: 'So that if you were to take five pieces of your own hair and look at that under a microscope, you might well not be able to say that they were from the same head?'

Peabody: 'I just don't know; it would depend which five hairs you chose.'

Lawrence: 'But if they were of different size, whatever, as hairs tend to be on anyone's head, you would not be able to say that they were from the same head?'
Peabody: 'I might be able to, but I could not say that. I cannot until I have seen the hairs that you are hypothesising upon.'
Lawrence: 'But we are not talking about "mights", you see, we are talking about certainties.'
Peabody: 'Mmm.'

Dr Peabody, it seemed, could not be sure about anything and Lawrence was making a meal out of his 'maybes'. Lawrence flicked through his papers and accepted a note of instruction from Ralph Haeems. He took a sip of water, carefully put the plastic cup down and began to question Peabody about the 'Pinto' tradename.

Lawrence: 'Has your laboratory tried on your behalf to track down the source of the "Pinto" to see how many there are in circulation in Brighton today?'
Peabody: 'We have made a trace of the index mark at our disposal and we have not found the source of the "Pinto" trademark.'
Lawrence: 'I suppose that if they were on sale in the street market they would not find their way into the trademarks?'
Peabody: 'If "Pinto" was just made up, no.'

Lawrence soon established that the prosecution had no knowledge of who made the 'Pinto', where they made it, where it might have been sold or to whom. My research showed that it had been sold at a local market and that a pair of black slip-on shoes was sold to the same customer.

There was one other kind of hair found on the three garments under closest examination – ivy hairs. Their identification was confirmed by Dr David Cutler at the Jodrell Laboratory, Royal Botanical Gardens, Kew, where Dr Peabody and Detective Inspector Bentham visited him on 7 November 1986. Peabody made the comment that although ivy is a relatively common plant, the epidermal hairs are not normally encountered on clothing. In fact, he went one step further. He did not recall ever seeing them present on clothing before. As he had examined thousands of garments worn by victims and offenders alike, the presence of these tiny hairs on three sweatshirts attributed to two victims and a killer was clearly more than coincidence.

On his return to Aldermaston, Dr Peabody examined Nicola's clothing and tapings from her body and found a total of 1120 epidermal ivy hairs. On Karen's clothing and body tapings he found a total of 1468 epidermal ivy hairs. He then examined the 'Pinto' sweatshirt and found a total of 670 epidermal ivy hairs. He also examined the boiler suit he himself had worn to the scene of the crime and found only 39 ivy hairs. What he didn't do and what I did was to calculate the amounts of ivy hairs adhering to just the three sweatshirts: 421 on Nicola's, 720 on Karen's and 670 on the 'Pinto'. Both the defence and prosecution forensic scientists agreed that this amount of foliage could only have become attached to the garments in a manner consistent with heavy, rough contact having occurred. The defence later argued in court that the 'Pinto' had been found in an area where ivy grew in abundance and contended that the contamination of the garment could have occurred when it was discarded or kicked about. I believe that the similarity in the numbers of hairs found on the sweatshirts is significant, but unfortunately no such breakdown was aired before the jury.

*　　*　　*

The 'Pinto' sweatshirt had carried some red staining and tests were undertaken to establish whether the stain compound matched any substances removed from Bishop's house.

Bishop worked from time to time on a number of cars, his own and those belonging to friends like Michael Evans at 19 Medmery Hill, Brighton, and Geoffrey Caswell at 24 Stephen's Road. Bishop at that time had a red Ford Escort (MGX 681P) and a red Ford Cortina (XMC 403 T) and Caswell had a maroon Mini saloon (UMC 883 M).

Stephen Fenner, the scenes of crime investigator in 1986, had decided to miss the local Guy Fawkes night celebrations and at 7 p.m. he went to Michael Evans' home to carry out an examination of the driveway and garage at the rear of the premises. He took away several paint samples from both before he came across a piece of masking tape with paint adhering to it. He labelled it SJF/70.

Edward Redman early that November had decided to re-visit the Bishops' home yet again. He had noticed that several of the outhouse doors in the alleyway had been sprayed about waist-high with red paint in graffiti style. He removed samples of red paint from six of the doors – 15, 19, 21, 23, 25 and 27. No paint was found on Bishop's outhouse door, number 17. Redman went off in search of the spray gun he had seen on an earlier visit, but it had mysteriously disappeared, never to be seen again. He did then decant some red paint from a container found in Bishop's outhouse into a specimen jar which he labelled EWR/72. The police had traced the broken-down car Bishop had sold for £50 to John Hazel. Although he had already dismantled the vehicle and sold various parts, Redman removed several samples of paint from the wing mirror, a right-side door and from the inside of the same door.

During October and November 1986, David Burt, another forensic scientist at Aldermaston, received an impressive number of items for chemical examination:

DE/1	Blue 'Pinto' sweatshirt
JNJ/1	Blue/grey trousers
SJF/51	Tin of cellulose primer
EWR/72	Contents of JGP/1, a tin of paint
EWR/73	Red paint from round the door mirror of Bishop's Ford Escort
EWR/74	Red paint from a right-side door of Bishop's Ford Escort
EWR/75	Red paint off the inside of the same door
SJF/53	Red paint from the offside wing of Bishop's Ford Escort
SJF/60	Red paint from the bonnet of Bishop's Ford Escort
SJF/67	Red paint from the radiator grille of Bishop's Ford Escort
SJF/68	Paint from the garage wall, 19 Medmery Hill
SJF/70	Paint on tape from the garage floor, 19 Medmery Hill
RT/3	Paint from the offside wing of Caswell's Mini saloon
RT/7	Paint from the nearside wing of Caswell's Mini saloon
RT/13	Paint from the roof gully of Caswell's Mini saloon
EWR/108	Tin of Turtle Wax polish (drop of paint on lid)
EWR/110	Red paint from the bonnet of Bishop's Ford Cortina
EWR/112	Red paint from the vent grille under the windscreen of Bishop's Ford Cortina

EWR/128   Piece of rag with red stains (found in Newick
          Road)
EWR/78   Paint from outhouse door, 19 Stephen's Road
EWR/79   Paint from outhouse door, 21 Stephen's Road
EWR/80   Paint from outhouse door, 23 Stephen's Road
EWR/81   Paint from outhouse door, 25 Stephen's Road
EWR/82   Paint from outhouse door, 27 Stephen's Road
JSM/2   Paint container from 19 Medmery Hill

There were two types and colour of paint found on the 'Pinto' – one bright red, the other maroon.

The red paint from the outhouse doors was an extremely thin coat and it was therefore difficult to make an accurate colour comparison with the red paint found on the 'Pinto' and on Bishop's trousers. However, chemical similarities were found between the red paint on the 'Pinto' and the paint from the doors numbered 19 and 21 (EWR/78 and EWR/79). Even considering the poor nature of the samples from the doors, Dr Burt could not rule out the possibility that these paints came from the same source. EWR/110, the red topcoat from the bonnet of Bishop's Ford Cortina, did match the red paint found on the 'Pinto' and the outhouse doors in almost every respect in colour, microscopic appearance and chemical composition.

Bishop has consistently denied having sprayed the outhouse doors himself. I interviewed him on a number of occasions at his home and he admitted that some young children took a spray gun belonging to him and used it to spray these doors. This could be substantiated by the fact that the graffiti reached only to adult waist height: children could reach no higher. This spray gun went missing, never to be found.

The following items contained maroon paint matching

that on the 'Pinto' in colour, microscopic appearance and chemical composition:

RT/3	Offside wing, Caswell's Mini saloon
RT/7	Second layer of paint from nearside front wing of Caswell's Mini saloon
RT/13	Roof gully of Caswell's mini saloon
SJF/70	Maroon paint adhering to masking tape from 19 Medmery Hill
EWR/108	Maroon paint adhering to the inner surface of the lid of the Turtle Wax tin in the form of dried droplet
JSM/2	Maroon paint deposits on the spray paint container bowl found at 19 Medmery Hill (used to hold the paint)

The maroon paint top coat from the nearside front wing of the Mini matched that of the sample of Damask Red 'Car Plan' spray paint (SLC/1) found at Bishop's home. Clearly, whoever wore the 'Pinto' had also worked on Caswell's car.

Bright red paint deposits were found on the blue-grey trousers (JNJ/1), but were different in chemical composition from the bright red paint found on the 'Pinto'. The items of red paint that matched the trousers in colour, microscopic appearance and chemical composition were:

SJF/53	Red top coat from the offside front wing of Bishop's Ford Escort
SJF/60	Red top coat from the bonnet of Bishop's Ford Escort
SJF/67	Red paint from the radiator grille of Bishop's Ford Escort
SJF/68	Red paint from the wall, 19 Medmery Hill
EWR/128	Red paint from the rag found in Newick Road

JSM/2   Red paint found on the spray paint container (which was also contaminated with the maroon paint)

Burt was unable to establish a link between the clothing and the samples taken from:

SJF/51   Tin of cellulose primer
EWR/72   Paint content of jar (JPG/1)
EWR/73   Red paint from the door mirror of Bishop's Ford Escort
EWR/74   Red paint from the right-side mirror of Bishop's Ford Escort
EWR/75   Red paint from the inside of door of Bishop's Ford Escort
EWR/81   Red paint from outhouse door numbers 23/25/27.

Evans stated that Bishop had used his garage to spray motor vehicles and Caswell stated that Bishop had helped him to spray his Mini. To judge from the matches made between the site, the paints, the 'Pinto' and the trousers, there were clear links to Bishop. Paint samples from his scrapped Ford Escort matched samples from the garage wall at Medmery Hill, from the paint container and from the lint rag found near the Fellows home in Newick Road – the very road Bishop and others had walked along on the day of the murders. All these are linked to the 'Pinto' as well, and the paint on the rag also matched that on the blue-grey trousers. Bishop's contact with the rag, the paint container and the masking tape is significant.

It was argued most effectively by the defence at the trial that there was no evidence to suggest that Bishop could have worn his blue-grey trousers and his alleged 'Pinto' sweatshirt at the same time while spraying cars, as there was an absence of fine spray droplets on either garment. To support their theory, the defence claimed that the paint found on both the 'Pinto' and the blue-grey trousers, in the form of a mass and not a fine spray, was inconsistent with car-spraying but consistent with paint having been rubbed on or wiped across them. The prosecution suggested that both garments could have been worn together while rubbing-down work was in progress on a car, with the contamination being localised to specific areas, as indeed it was.

The paint mark on the cuff of the 'Pinto' was acquired when the Ford Escort was being prepared with a rubbing-down compound prior to spraying. Bishop admits that he rubbed the car down in a public car park in Brighton's town centre and that several people, including Marion Stevenson, were there when he did so. He still denies that the 'Pinto' was his or that he wore it.

During the research for this book two other individuals positively identified the 'Pinto' as belonging to Bishop but having been worn by another man on several occasions. I dutifully passed on this vital information to the Crown Prosecution Service.

The Paint Evidence

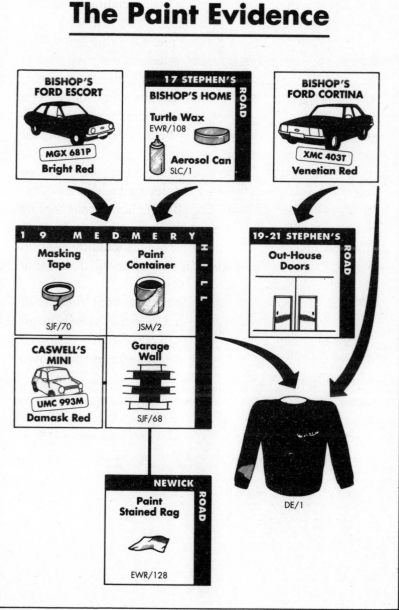

BISHOP'S FORD ESCORT
MGX 681P
Bright Red

17 STEPHEN'S ROAD
BISHOP'S HOME
Turtle Wax
EWR/108
Aerosol Can
SLC/1

BISHOP'S FORD CORTINA
XMC 403T
Venetian Red

19 MEDMERY HILL
Masking Tape
SJF/70
Paint Container
JSM/2
CASWELL'S MINI
UMC 993M
Damask Red
Garage Wall
SJF/68

19-21 STEPHEN'S ROAD
Out-House Doors

NEWICK ROAD
Paint Stained Rag
EWR/128

DE/1

12. Evidence and Questions: 3

Dr Peabody, in his examination of the murdered girls' clothing, had discovered no semen on any of the swabs or articles labelled 'Hadaway'. Karen's T-shirt was smeared with blood on the front, with vomit at the right front; vomit was also present on the right shoulder and lower back. The green sweatshirt was generally in good condition and no blood or vomit was found on this garment (EWR/10). The knickers, now labelled EWR/9, were generally well worn but undamaged, though there was an area of blood smearing on the back of them. Karen's stomach contents consisted of a small amount of a semi-dark liquid, consistent with a 'Tip-Top' drink, a small fragment of meat and part of either a bean or a pea – probably the remains of her school dinner.

No semen was found on any of the swabs or articles of clothing labelled 'Fellows'. Nicola's pink T-shirt (EWR/37) had bloodstaining on both shoulders, on the right front and right sleeve. The blood on the shoulders appeared to be mixed with vomit. There was no bloodstaining on her vest (IEW/38), skirt (IEW/39) or on her knickers (IEW/40), though there was faecal staining on the outside of the crotch area of this garment. The stomach contents consisted of a mass of partially digested food with the appearance of chips and some meat fragments.

Cross-examination of Dr Peabody on these subjects was very revealing.

Lawrence: 'Can you help us about Karen's pants, EWR/9. There was an area of blood smearing on the back of her knickers?'
Peabody: 'Yes.'
Lawrence: 'Were there any bloodstains on her behind or bleeding from her vagina?'
Mr Justice Schiemann: 'Did you examine her body?'
Peabody: 'I did not, my lord.'
Lawrence: 'You would have wanted to examine, would you not, the blood on the knickers to see if that were Karen's blood or blood of the attacker?'
Peabody: 'I did not.'
Lawrence: 'Why not?'
Peabody: 'One might assume the girl might have been injured – she has blood on the back of her knickers. It is an assumption that the blood comes from her.'
Lawrence: 'I suggest, and I suggest on the basis of the evidence which we have not yet heard, that there was no bloodstaining on her anus or bleeding from her vagina. If that is so, there would be significance in bloodstaining on the pants which it was not immediately obvious came from her?'

This was a confused and extremely roundabout way of putting a question. Nicola was sexually assaulted twice from behind and did lose blood; she was found wearing knickers that were not bloodstained. Karen wore no knickers on discovery of her body and those attributed to her were bloodstained. I suggest that the killer replaced Karen's undergarments on to Nicola and left Nicola's, which were bloodstained, on the ground, later to be attributed to Karen. Lawrence was seeking to discredit the witness and to show that the prosecution had failed in their duty to undertake tests that might eliminate his client from suspicion of murder.

Questioned again on the bloodstained knickers, Peabody replied, 'If one had grouped it, one might have known who it was from.'

Lawrence: 'Was the blood on the pants ever grouped?'
Peabody: 'No, it was not. I have already said that.'
Lawrence: 'Bishop gave you his blood or gave the police surgeon his blood. It could have been compared and what you are saying is, it was not?'
Peabody: 'There was an area of a little amount of staining on the back. I suspect there may not have been enough for a try. One might have had a try had it been thought necessary.'

The 'little amount' of bloodstaining Peabody refers to covers an area of $3\frac{1}{2}$ by $4\frac{1}{2}$ inches.

Lawrence: 'Somebody thought it was not necessary to group the blood on the pants to see if it could be connected with Bishop or any suspect?'
Peabody: 'It was assumed the blood on the back of her knickers was hers.'

There was no injury on Karen that could have supported the presence of blood on her undergarments. There was on Nicola.

Lawrence: 'Even if there was no sign of blood coming from the vagina or the anus?'
Peabody: 'I did not know that.'

Peabody's lack of knowledge of the pathologist's report of the post-mortem was very surprising. As it was, the possible exchange of undergarments slipped through the net.

Vital trace evidence had not even been looked at and no attempt was made to link or dismiss Bishop from connection with it.

The defence made much of the fact that no body or environmental temperatures were taken, linking this not just to the time of death but to the idea that the girls had been killed elsewhere and brought to the den within an hour or two of death. In addition they were critical of the way the girls' injuries had been examined. In reaching conclusions, it should be remembered that all the Callans had had to work from were the scenes of crime photographs and Dr West's report: any defence scientist is at the disadvantage of having to rely on the judgement of someone else and to obtain information secondhand.

Callan mentioned a bruise on the front of Karen's neck, which appeared to measure 4 by 2½ inches. He wrote:

'This is very characteristic of the palm of a hand (together and in juxtaposition with finger-bruising as in the photo 5). The hand mark is almost certainly made from behind the victim. The mark is therefore of a right hand, the grip is from behind, the thumb to the right of the chin and the fingers to the left of the chin. The size of 4" × 2½" would not really give a useful idea as to the size of the hand except in the most general terms . . .

'I am unable to visualise the exact position of the neck bruising without detailed photographs (in conjunction with the post-mortem description), but there seems to have been no work carried out in trying to determine the size of the hand marks on the necks and whether it was predominantly left or right . . . I consider that two very serious areas of omission by the police scenes of crime were that they appeared not:

1. To try and have the skin of the neck area fingerprinted.
2. To ensure that the neck areas were photographed in

order that subcutaneous bruising may assist with "sizing" the hand(s) which caused the strangulation.'

Professor Derrick J. Pounder is one of the world's leading experts in the field of forensic pathology. He spent several years as a specialist pathologist at the Institute of Medical and Veterinary Science, Adelaide, South Australia, and Senior Lecturer (forensic pathology) at the University of Adelaide. He was also Deputy Chief Medical Examiner, Edmonton, Canada, and Associate Professor in the Department of Pathology at the University of Alberta and the University of Calgary. He is currently Professor of Forensic Medicine at the University of Dundee. He has this to say about 'sizing':

'As far as measurements of the external marks were concerned, these can be used to estimate the span of the hand. Such measurements are clearly not precise but can be helpful in eliminating, rather than incriminating suspects. Some measurements of this should have been made by the pathologist. I assume that the individual marks were all measured by the pathologist, since this would be a routine part of any medico-legal autopsy. Reconstructing measurements from two-dimensional photographs taken at the time of autopsy is prone to error because of the distortion which arises in producing a two-dimensional photograph from a three-dimensional object.'

No attempt was made to size the marks referred to by Callan; and Dr Richard Gray, the deputy police surgeon who made such a thorough examination of Bishop, did not take detailed measurements of Bishop's hands. Of course, it might be argued that Bishop's fingerprints and palm prints were taken by the police later and that these would have given an indication of his hand size, but no attempt was made to compare Bishop's hand size with the marks round Karen's neck. An opportunity to eliminate or confirm him as a suspect was missed.

The 'Pinto' sweatshirt was the linchpin, such as it was, in the prosecution case. Although a number of people had come forward to say it belonged to Bishop, these statements had by now resolved themselves to a very different 'I thought it belonged to Bishop.' No one saw him wearing it on 9 October 1986, indeed there are statements that support Bishop's claim that he was wearing a blue sweatshirt with a red and white stripe across the chest.

Lawrence was clearly unhappy over the way the garments had been handled from the outset and attempted to imply that some degree of cross-contamination could have occurred either at the police station or at the laboratory. He discovered that the 'Pinto' had been wrapped, un-wrapped, stretched over a cardboard frame, un-wrapped and re-wrapped so many times that no one could accept responsibility for its condition when it first arrived on Peabody's table. Peabody explained the procedure adopted for the examination of articles at Aldermaston. Each item is placed on to a freshly scrubbed table. No other items are examined together on the same table, even in the same room, on occasions. An article was taken out of its bag and replaced into the same bag after examination. This was always the case and there were no exceptions. The problem with the 'Pinto's' condition seemed to have been caused by the police.

Mr Justice Schiemann began his summing-up to the jury on 9 December 1987, a task he completed fairly, keeping an open mind regarding the chances of a successful appeal for Bishop if he were to be convicted. It was a model summing-up.

The jury retired to consider their verdict at 10.38 a.m. and returned to the court at 12.45 p.m. with a unanimous verdict of 'Not Guilty'. There was uproar. Russell Bishop collapsed sobbing while ecstatic relations fought a pitched battle with police officers. There were shouts, screams and scuffles and two women jurors burst into tears. Extra police were drafted in to restore order. Immediately after the verdict, the police took the unprecedented step of publicly stating: 'We are not looking for anybody else unless we receive new information, which we believe is unlikely. That is it. Closed. No more enquiries.'

After the court emptied, Lee Hadaway stood with his distraught wife. The police officer in charge had pushed past them without a word. Lee said between tears, 'Someone must have killed our baby. Now it seems we'll never know.'

13. The Criminal Justice System

Several issues should be raised for debate as a result of the 1986 Russell Bishop trial. The adversarial system of English justice is exemplified by this trial, where the aim seems to be not so much to find the truth but to determine whether or not the prosecution can prove its case beyond reasonable doubt. It is in this context that the ability of the defence to prove and challenge scientific evidence in particular is seriously questioned, not only because such evidence may prove difficult of access but because of the inequality of resources to finance the work. Writing about the criminal justice system in the *Guardian* in 1989, Clare Wood commented on the ethics of the police, which is to secure conviction, adding, '. . . the police are free to formulate an early theory of guilt and pursue evidence with a blinkered disregard for other explanations.' Might this have happened in the Wild Park investigation?

The principle of English justice allows that an accused person is innocent until proven guilty. Only the most naive individual would believe that this ensures a fair submission of evidence by the prosecution balanced by an offer of full facilities and shared information with the defence. In practice, Bishop would most likely have been found guilty in 1986 had his advisers, Mr and Mrs Callan, taken the perfunctory fee to which they were entitled for a one-hour examination of the forensic evidence. As Mr

Callan put it, 'We could have gone home after making everyone happy by agreeing with the prosecution.' Might there be justification for thinking that on occasions this is exactly what happens?

Clearly, Callan was extremely worried about the evidence against Bishop, which was selective in the extreme. It was inevitable that the question of money should enter into the reckoning: while the prosecution could spend £1¼ million on the case in an effort to convict Bishop – Callan estimated that Aldermaston alone spent about £40,000 – resources of a similar kind were not available to keep Bishop, who at this stage was an innocent person, out of prison. It is nonetheless significant that Bishop, with the help of a solicitor, about £4000 from the Legal Aid Fund and three days' work by an allegedly hampered pair of forensic advisers, was able to protect himself from conviction.

Callan even went to the trouble of suggesting that Ralph Haeems should instigate an enquiry into the fact that the police did not examine items of clothing, or even take clothing, from other individuals who featured prominently in the initial investigation. He said, 'Unless all the suggested work is carried out and understood, the defendant cannot get a fair trial and I foresee that he will not, purely as a matter of cost. One is working at a considerable disadvantage by comparison to the prosecution, who in practice have unlimited resources.' He went on to make a suggestion:

'If I were to have a totally free hand I would advocate that I re-submit all the exhibits again to a different government laboratory . . . The method of using another government forensic laboratory would probably be cheapest in the long run as it would be a government paying a government, and the very best facilities are available.' Callan is referring to the Legal Aid System paying a government body, not a commercial laboratory.

'However, the politics may be impossible to resolve. If it were possible, I would like to undertake the actual laboratory form submission, in order that we could direct the laboratory work in a more "neutral" mode. I am aware that what I suggest is totally unprecedented in the United Kingdom. I know that it is going to cost a very large amount of money. I know it constitutes a very considerable time delay in coming to trial. I am, however, of the opinion that unless something is done to get into the deeper reaches of this case, it would have been better if we had never started . . . I am sorry to give you these enormously complex problems but I am very disturbed about what we have seemed to have found so far. In my opinion, the uncontested acceptance of the prosecution scientific/technical evidence in this case would indeed be most unsafe.'

If Callan's conclusions were to be acted on, they indeed would have far-reaching effects upon the English legal system. Serious moral and ethical issues are at stake. Bishop was, after all, at that stage, an innocent man fighting for his freedom. Ranged against him were the entire resources of the Sussex Constabulary, countless experienced officers and modern technology in the form of computerisation and advanced forensic science techniques acknowledged by many to be the best in the world. Yet even with these resources elementary mistakes were made.

At the beginning of the murder hunt, experienced officers were drafted in to assist, but within a matter of days many of them with first-hand experience of the case were returned to their previous duties. To fill their places dozens of special constables were brought in to carry out

routine house-to-house enquiries. While there can be no
criticism of the commitment of these part-time
policemen, it is readily agreed by many professional
officers that they are inadequately trained for tasks such
as that of knocking on doors at the Moulsecoomb Estate
and being confronted by inhabitants with strong anti-
police sentiments. Such was the nature of their results
that full-time officers then had to duplicate this laborious
task.

During the course of researching this book, out of
courtesy I asked if the Sussex police wished to make any
contribution. The official reply came from J. D. Dibley,
Assistant Chief Constable, which thanked me for my letter and concluded by saying that the Sussex police could
not supply details of their investigation.

On 10 April 1989 I wrote a detailed letter to the then
Home Secretary, The Rt Hon Douglas Hurd MP. One of
the issues raised was the return of Karen's clothes to her
parents. It was a delicate matter that the family had
wished to resolve and had indeed attempted to achieve for
some years. I drafted a formal letter for them. Their
daughter's effects were returned in a black dustbin liner.

Another issue raised concerned a previous enquiry into
the prosecution's conduct throughout the case. The Home
Secretary declined to reply personally. Instead, an open
letter was received from the Director of Public Prosecutions at the offices of the Crown Prosecution Service in
Queen Anne's Gate. One question was answered as follows: 'I can confirm that the Director of Public Prosecutions enquired into the conduct of the prosecution of
the case and that enquiry was completed by 12 December
1988. Certain matters were raised in February 1989 but
by 5 April all enquiries had been completed.' The CPS
gave no indication of the result of these 'enquiries' yet the

bitter irony of the whole case is that the police will not re-open enquiries unless substantial new evidence is forth-coming from a member of the tax-paying public. The sug-gestion to me was to go out and get the information and we might look into it.

The forensic science service did little to enhance its reputation by its role in this case. Like the police service, it too is under great pressure to produce results. To a certain extent, its success in developing new methods of detection has itself helped to increase that pressure: in the public view, techniques such as DNA finger-printing are perceived as infallible, so great store has been set on the ability of science to catch criminals.

Cracks in the system first became evident in the 1970s when the evidence of a Home Office forensic scientist, which helped to convict John Preece of murder, was found to be unreliable. The conviction was quashed on appeal and Preece was freed after serving nine years in prison. A review of the forensic science service followed and it was acknowledged that scientists were working under great strain to deal with an ever-increasing workload while being pressed to produce fast results. Critics pointed out that this was surely a recipe for mistakes, and doubts began to surface about the safety of other convictions obtained on the strength of forensic evidence. In 1977 quality assur-ance was introduced and strenuous attempts made to standardise the procedures used in Britain's six regional crime laboratories. Unfortunately, some earlier convic-tions did prove controversial and surfaced later to haunt the forensic service. The evidence against the Maguire family in relation to the Guildford pub bombings in 1974 was discredited, and the safety of the conviction of the so-called Birmingham Six has been so seriously challenged that they have since been released after a series of appeals.

Forensic pathology also felt under pressure, as their 30 practitioners covering the country have to deal with similar problems: they face an increasing workload against a background of poor mortuary facilities and cuts in university funding which threaten future training. In 1984, commenting on the shortage of trained pathologists, Professor Bernard Knight was reported as saying, 'The day is going to come when the police find a body in a muddy field and no one will be there to come and help them.'

In 1988 there were criticisms of delays in carrying out routine forensic testing in London, with 26 weeks cited for analysing a drug sample. Press reports talked of a system which was crippling the courts. Further unease was expressed in 1990 by senior figures who had left the forensic service to set out in private practice. They talked about some of the weaknesses inherent in the system, particularly with reference to the needs of defence lawyers. There was concern about the ability of defence witnesses to challenge scientific evidence and of courts to understand much of the sophisticated interpretation desired from it.

Under the present system of criminal justice, it is the prosecution which holds the trump cards from the very beginning. The Home Office laboratories are a public service and are supposed to assist the defence when called upon. In practice, this rarely happens because by the time the defence advisers arrive on the scene, the investigative trail has either gone cold or has been thoroughly surveyed by the prosecution, so that interpretation is the only issue. Not surprisingly, defence advisers are reluctant to submit new material for examination because the system requires this to be done through the police investigating officer.

When access is given to forensic materials in the Home

Office laboratories, the decreed co-operation may be grudging, if not hostile, as alleged by the Callans in the Babes in the Wood case. Because of the manner in which the system operates, favouring the prosecution, dissidents from the forensic science service say that some innocent persons have been found guilty – this, of course, is not a matter of supposition; it is public knowledge. It would be equally true to say that some who are guilty are never brought to justice. Most damning of all is that a system which is rarely available to the defence anyway, is, in the event, not adequately understood in terms of the growing sophistication of scientific evidence. Part-time defence experts drawn from the universities or other institutions simply cannot match the experience and knowledge of the professionals working in the forensic science service. As it happened, what case there was against Bishop in 1986/7 collapsed in an untidy heap of muddled paperwork and wasted effort. Critics of this book might well argue that the system worked despite the imbalance of finance and investigative resources. Others might say that because of negligence and incompetence the prosecution allowed a double killer to walk free.

It certainly seemed as if exercising their right to examine the evidence proved difficult for the defence. The suggestion that documents and photographs were initially withheld, and statements about the repressive working conditions that the Callans allege were eventually won from the Aldermaston forensic science service, raise troubling questions. Callan commented, 'I find this type of evidence most disturbing as, while telling the truth, it does not tell the whole truth, because it makes forensic examinations selective, dependent on what one is trying to prove.' Regarding the photographs, he claimed in a letter to Bishop's solicitor: 'As you know, during our first visit to Aldermaston I was not permitted to see any of the police photographs. I was subsequently permitted to see the photographs for the first time on 1 October, that was the only time. Indeed, even up until receipt of the albums from you, I was only aware of the two post-mortem albums and the one scenes of crime album. I did not know the others existed: they were never referred to me in any way.'

As a matter of courtesy, I submitted the defence complaints to the director at Aldermaston and to Detective Chief Superintendent Christopher Page of the Sussex police for their comment. Chief Superintendent Page admitted that the matter raised 'deep moral and ethical issues'. Indeed it does and when it is borne in mind that the 'selection by direction' process proved so faulty in this case, the rush to judgement is indefensible.

Under these conditions justice becomes a lottery. Ludovic Kennedy, the celebrated author, broadcaster and crime writer, summed it up neatly:

'Let no one pretend that our system of justice is a search for the truth. It is nothing of the kind. It is a contest between both sides played according to certain rules, and if the truth happens to emerge as a result of the contest, then it is pure windfall. But it is unlikely to. It is not something with which the contestants are concerned. They are concerned only that the game should be played according to the rules. There are many rules and one of them is that some questions which might provide a short cut to the truth are not allowed to be asked, and those that are asked are not allowed to be answered. The result is that results are often reached haphazardly, for the wrong reasons, in spite of the evidence, and may or may not coincide with the literal truth. The tragedy of our courts is that means have come to count for more than ends, form more than content, appearance more than reality. The antique ritual is positively harmful, for it drives a wedge between the citizen and the law, outlawing him as a stranger in his own land . . .'

The reply from Mr Neylan at Aldermaston is quoted in full:

'HOME OFFICE FORENSIC SCIENCE LABORATORY
Aldermaston Reading Berkshire RG7 4PN

Mr Christopher Berry-Dee	Your reference
	Our reference DN/PJT-Casework
	Date 11 August 1989

Dear Mr Berry-Dee

Re: HADAWAY Karen & FELLOWS Nicola (Homicide ×
2) 9 October 1986 Brighton

I do not intend to deal in every minute particular with the issues raised by your letter of 8 July, but I want to place on record a number of points concerning the procedures for the defence analysis of forensic evidence.

As someone who is acquainted with the Criminal Justice system, I am sure you will know that there are basic rules governing the assistance which is offered to the defence. The rules were formalised two years ago, but have been in general operation for many years. The rules entitle both the defence and prosecution to see all records of work, etc, which underly the expert evidence to be produced by the other side, and for the defence to make its own examination of any item. However, it is utterly forbidden for the defence to go on what the courts call "fishing expeditions". These rules have been laid down by the judiciary, and not by the laboratory.

Over many years this laboratory has gained considerable

experience of giving assistance to those experts employed
by the defence. Our assistance has always been given
openly. Indeed, our assistance usually goes beyond that
which is required by the judicial rules – though we do
remain, of course, within the bounds of propriety.

This case was no exception – it is utterly untrue to claim
that the laboratory did not cooperate.

In investigations which involve the examination of
many hundreds of items, such as this one, it is always
established beforehand which items are of interest to the
defence expert. This is long established practice. The
defence are entitled to examine any item they wish, without constraint, and to see the relevant papers. In simple
cases the laboratory will normally arrange for every exhibit to be made available, but in a case like this it is clearly
pointless to arrange for the production of van loads of
items in which the defence has no interest. The decision
on which evidence to examine is obviously a matter for
the defence, in consultation with their expert adviser(s).
On this occasion we were asked by the defence to produce
three items. We did so.

You will of course know that once a laboratory has
made its examination, items are returned to the custody
of the police. If the items are required again they have to
be brought back by police. This is not possible at the drop
of a hat, particularly when the items are stored in
Brighton, some distance away from the laboratory at
Aldermaston. Had the defence expert required to see
further items this should have been agreed beforehand
with the defence and then arrangements would have
been made with the police. Given reasonable notice we
will willingly provide any item which is requested.
Indeed, on this and all subsequent occasions in this case,
the laboratory responded to every defence request.

Many of the matters raised in Mr Callan's letter, for instance the supposed withholding of evidence and alleged unhelpfulness of police officers, are not the responsibility of the laboratory and should be properly addressed to the defence solicitor, defence expert or to the police. I am quite obviously not in a position to speak for them.

It is interesting to note, and of course you are aware of it, since you are in possession of a subsequent letter sent by Mr Callan to the defence solicitors, that the defence expert endorsed the evidential work carried out by the laboratory in this case. In his words the "results and conclusions . . . are irrefutably correct".

As I have pointed out in previous correspondence, the laboratory is not in a position to comment any further on this case. I must also state, once again, that at no time did the laboratory offer anything but the fullest co-operation with the defence experts in accordance with the court rules. There is not and never has been any question of impropriety in the way in which the laboratory carried out the forensic work in this case. To suggest otherwise is without foundation, and we would have to consider what response would be appropriate if such allegations were made.

Yours sincerely

D. Neylan
Director

Copies to: Mr R. Payne – Public Relations Branch
Det. Ch. Supt. Hills – Sussex Police
Dr J. Thompson – Director General – FSS
H.O. Legal Department
CPS – Mr David Thompson – Chief Crown Prosecutor – Sussex

Callan certainly did make a very significant remark in a letter dated apparently 2 October 1987 (the date is somewhat erased by over-type). He says on page 4 para 2:

'We are totally convinced that Dr Peabody's results and conclusions relating to the fibre exchange, and therefore association of all items as in the sketch attached, are irrefutably correct i.e. there is extremely strong evidence that at some time the "Pinto" sweatshirt has been in contact with all these items:

Hadaway's sweatshirt, T-shirt and skirt

Fellows' sweatshirt

Bishop's trousers

Stevenson's skirt

This logically proves only two things:

(a) Stevenson knows who owned or used the "Pinto" sweatshirt

(b) Bishop knows who owned or used the "Pinto" sweatshirt'

Callan continued: 'In order to get such vital information as they undoubtedly have, it is imperative that they be told that knowledge of, or even ownership of the sweatshirt, does not imply guilt of the offence.'

It is known that a small circle of Bishop's friends were engaging in car renovation and re-spraying with him; any of these could have worn the 'Pinto' sweatshirt. One of that group, or a close associate, could have killed the two girls. If the crime was not committed by one of them, someone in that group knew who owned the 'Pinto' or could have found out. Not one of them came forward to assist the murder enquiry.

Marion Stevenson has been interviewed by me on a number of occasions. She has said that there was something about that terrible evening of 9 October 1986 that she cannot recall, that it has been erased from her mind.

She has also identified a wearer of the 'Pinto'. That man was not Bishop.

Bishop was asked by me in the presence of witnesses if he could assist in identifying the 'Pinto' and the person to whom it belonged or who wore it. He made a startling claim that he had attempted to identify the wearer (not the owner) of the 'Pinto' during his time in custody, a claim that has since been verified. Bishop's legal advisers decided to keep this information to themselves, thinking that Bishop's claim might not be treated seriously by the police to whom he was known to have lied. Bishop then explained to me again in the presence of witnesses how the paint came to be on the 'Pinto's' cuff and who was wearing the garment when the work was carried out, thus providing a secondary link to the person identified by Marion Stevenson. Callan then went on to provide a list of individuals who fitted the identities of possible wearers/owners of the 'Pinto'. The list is short, with four names.

A number of witnesses gave statements to the police indicating that Bishop was the owner of the 'Pinto', yet not one of them was called to give evidence at the trial. I have interviewed several individuals who have told me in front of an independent witness that the sweatshirt was worn by another person. One of these new witnesses volunteered the information that the wearer suffered a BO problem. Bishop did not suffer from BO. Subsequently, I located two other individuals never previously interviewed by the police. Apart from giving vital new evidence, they both positively identified the wearer of the 'Pinto'. It was not Bishop. They did not even know Bishop by sight.

It is possible that if the police had not been so single-minded in pursuing Russell Bishop, they might have opened their minds to other possibilities. Reading two of the witnesses' depositions makes it clear that error had crept into the police investigations. Had detectives checked out these discrepancies and interviewed the individuals concerned, the wearer of the 'Pinto' sweatshirt on 9 October would, in all probability, have been identified as an individual other than Bishop. The implications of that discovery would inevitably have led to fibre tapings being taken from that individual's clothing, which could have linked directly to the scene of the crime and to the victims' clothes. Further examination of the same statements would have proved a more reliable course of action than that pursued against Bishop.

As mentioned earlier, I reported my findings to the Crown Prosecution Service; the report was then studied by the Sussex police. No further action was taken – or at least the outcome of any investigation was not made known to me.

Epilogue

After his acquittal in the Babes in the Wood case Bishop celebrated with a bottle of champagne. He and Jennie Johnson booked into an hotel for the night. His 22-year-old brother Alec said, 'He's thrilled it's all over – but furious that a year of his life has been taken away by the police bungling. He was always innocent. We know that and most of Brighton feels the same way.' Most of Brighton perhaps, but not all. Russell Bishop's home in Stephen's Road was firebombed and leaflets naming him a 'child killer' were printed and distributed. Despite the hate campaign, he stayed in Brighton and it was the Hadaway and Fellows families who were eventually driven away, either by grief or by public hostility and vengefulness.

It was perhaps not surprising that when first approached by me, Bishop proved reluctant to co-operate. But in a unanimous expression of desire to assist in finding the murderer of the two little girls, all three families eventually helped in some degree. It took many months of painstaking effort to arrive at a point where the bereaved families felt able to talk about the case. The Hadaways now live in Surrey with their surviving children. On receipt of Karen's clothes from the Sussex police, they passed them to me with tears in their eyes. Their only wish is for the killer to be brought to justice. The Fellows family handed over an almost complete file which contained the sad photographs taken where the bodies were found. Because of their sensitive nature these pictures, taken by Mark Baynes, have been omitted from this book. The file was handed over to me in the knowledge that the statements made by Barrie Fellows and Douggie Judd to the police contain an account which was, to say the least, inconsistent with their other statements. From the descriptions in the press accounts of Barrie Fellows, he would seem to be a hard man, perhaps a bit of a bully, with an eye for a quick profit. As far as I am concerned, he has helped where he could and has never asked, nor does he expect, a penny for his co-operation. He has accepted that the book may prove disturbing to his family but he has said he is as anxious as anyone to see the killer brought to justice.

Sylvia Bishop passed over to me her diary and private notes about the case, which she had compiled during the initial investigation in an attempt to defend her son. Careful study of these papers shows her complete belief in Bishop's innocence as the killer of Karen and Nicola. Her brother, Michael Dawes, devoted a great deal of time and effort to the case. He is terminally ill and although confined to a wheelchair has spear-headed a campaign to have the case re-opened, and has convinced both Russell and Sylvia Bishop to help where they could with the research for this book. Michael opened many doors for me, offered much needed hospitality at times, employed the services of his own lawyer and spent hours painfully tapping out lengthy documents on his computer in a valiant attempt to assist in the compilation of this text.

As a result of such co-operation, *A Question of Evidence* is based on over a thousand official documents and photographs, combined with dozens of personal interviews with individuals wishing to put the record straight. Former Detective Sergeant Phil Swan, the officer who arrested and interviewed Bishop, now runs a public house in West Sussex. He is a former Royal Marine Commando and an officer in the elite Regional Crime Squad whose members are licensed to carry a firearm. He resigned from the force after the Babes in the Wood trial. It was not that he wanted to leave the police, but he felt he had become a scapegoat for his colleagues' mistakes, a discrepancy over a meal receipt. He is still bitter about the case, which he claims was 'botched'. He went on to tell me: 'I have been warned never to discuss the matter. If I do, then I run the risk of losing my publican's licence. They have ways of doing it, you know.'

Moulsecoomb has perhaps the highest record of serious sexual offences per square mile than any other council estate in the British Isles. At the time of writing, yet another rape has taken place there. The evil kidnapper, 23-year-old jobless Paul Burton, who abducted seven-year-old Gemma Lawrence from her holiday caravan in West Bay, Dorset, in August 1990, had also lived at Moulsecoomb. Jennie Johnson went to the same school as him and he knew Russell Bishop. Johnson claimed in the *Sun* newspaper on 14 February 1991 that Burton was always mean-looking and spoiling for a fight; he had drifted into crime after his parents split up. At Burton's trial, Judge Auld said that in Burton's own confession he had admitted indulging in sexual fantasies concerning young girls. Apart from abduction, Burton was also charged with indecent assault on Gemma and robbery, which involved hammering the head of a disabled retired heating engineer, 54-year-old Michael Edwards. Burton had then smothered the wheelchair-bound man with a pillow, after tying him up. Doctors claimed that Edwards was

lucky to be left alive. Burton was sent to Broadmoor, a
hospital for the criminally insane, with a life sentence.

Much of the information handed over to me was given
in complete confidence and therefore is not reproduced
here, but the information is not forgotten, nor has it been
wasted. A number of individuals interviewed during the
research for this book seemed to feel that they were under
suspicion, indeed several gave accounts which were at
variance with details they had previously given to the
Sussex Constabulary. I have no wish to exploit those
inconsistencies for the sake of sensational journalism, and
confidences therefore remain unbroken. Nevertheless,
what has been said has been checked and re-checked
where it strengthens doubts, uncertainties or omissions in
the police investigations.

Councillor Gordon J. Wingate, Labour representative for
the Moulsecoomb and Bevendean Ward, played an active
role in the sequel to the murders and Russell Bishop's
trial. A slightly built man who works as a porter at a local
hospital, Councillor Wingate has given much of his free
time campaigning to have the case re-opened, and for that
Brighton owes him and his family much gratitude.

In May 1989, Wingate wrote to the then Home Secretary, the Rt Hon Douglas Hurd MP, pointing out public
disquiet over the decision of the Sussex Constabulary not
to pursue their enquiries.

17 May 1989

'Dear Mr Hurd,
I am writing on behalf of Mr and Mrs Hadaway, the
parents of Karen Hadaway who, together with Nicola
Fellows, was tragically murdered in October 1986.

'As I am sure you are aware as Home Secretary, you

ordered an investigation into the murder trial held at Lewes Crown Court. It was anticipated that the investigation would take some four to six weeks, but it has now been fifteen months and still the bereaved family have not been given details of the investigation's findings, which leads me to say that this matter has been inadequately dealt with and has only added to the suffering of this family. Furthermore, in my letter to Lord McKay the Lord Chancellor to request the transcript of the trial [as the Hadaways obviously could not afford the fee of £4000, actually in excess of £10,000] I was informed that he could not be of assistance.

'Therefore, I do feel most strongly that in the course of natural justice Mr and Mrs Hadaway should not be denied the right to obtain the findings of the Home Office investigations and that these findings should be made public . . .

'Lastly, I feel sure that you can appreciate the disquiet felt by the residents of Moulsecoomb, where the children lived, and a very large proportion of the general public in Brighton, at the decision of the Sussex police not to pursue the enquiries further, and I am very concerned that it would appear that no one is likely to be brought to justice for these crimes.

Yours sincerely

Gordon Wingate (Cllr)'

Wingate waited for almost two months before he received the following reply from the Royal Courts of Justice dated 7 July 1989.

'Dear Councillor Wingate:

Your [sic] wrote to the Home Secretary on 17 March 1989 [date incorrect] on behalf of Mr and Mrs Hadaway, the parents of Karen Hadaway who, together with Nicola Fellows, was so tragically murdered in October 1986. The letter has been passed to me for reply because I have Ministerial responsibility for the work of the Crown Prosecution Service . . .

'I am of course aware of the concerns which have been expressed about the handling of the case against Russell Bishop, who was tried and acquitted at Lewes Crown Court. The inquiry to which you refer in the second paragraph of your letter was in fact instigated by the Director of Public Prosecutions himself as a direct response to the representations made to him; it was carried out under his personal supervision and thereafter he discussed the matter with me. The conclusion reached by the Director was that the case for the Crown was properly and competently prepared and presented by the very experienced Leading and Junior Counsel who appeared for the Prosecution, who took every step open to them within the rules of evidence to place before the jury all material to support the prosecution case. I emphasise that that conclusion was based on careful examinations of a review of all relevant material, and on consideration of representations made directly by relatives of Nicola Fellows and the solicitors acting on their behalf.

'At no time did the Director of Public Prosecutions envisage publication of the review on which his conclusions were based, and I am sure that nothing which he has said or done could have justified such an expectation. It is a fundamental principle of our system of justice that when a defendant has been acquitted by a court of competent jurisdiction, he face no further risk of conviction for the same offence. It would be wrong for the prosecuting authorities to publish a report going over much of the ground covered in the original trial, reopening issues which were concluded by the decision of the court.

'Further representations were subsequently made to

the Director, and on 22 February a meeting was convened at the Crown Prosecution Service Headquarters for the specific purpose of enabling additional points or representations to be made about the handling of the case. It was made clear at that stage that it would not be possible to enter into a dialogue about the details of the case, but the Director was anxious to ensure that no relevant material or considerations had been overlooked. The Director has continued to oversee the further enquiries and has personally considered the results thereof. He assures me that all the questions raised by the families of the murdered girls, and indeed every issue of any conceivable relevance to the case, have been most carefully considered by him, his staff and very experienced Counsel. He remains satisfied as to the handling of all aspects of the case.

'The families of both girls have my deepest sympathy, and I can understand their disappointment. I must tell you, however, that I am satisfied by the assurances which I have received from the Director personally, and accordingly I accept that he has acted quite correctly in deciding to conclude the matter.

'So far as the decision of the Sussex police not to pursue the enquiries further is concerned, that is a matter for the Chief Constable. However, the police made it clear that the decision was taken because they have no evidence on which to base further enquiries.

'Finally, you raised the point about the availability of the transcripts. The investigations carried out by the Director of Public Prosecutions made it necessary to obtain transcripts of significant passages of the evidence and summing up. Some of this material has already been supplied to Mr Heffron [Barrie Fellows's brother], who is interested on behalf of the families, and it would be a matter for the Director to whom I will send a copy of our

correspondence to make any further decision about any parts of the transcript which are in his possession.
Yours sincerely.'

The hardworking Councillor Wingate organised a public meeting in Brighton in 1989 at which I was asked to speak. Various disturbing aspects of the case were aired in public and the outcome probably ranks as a first in the annals of British crime. With generous cover by the media, the meeting decided to stage a protest march through the streets of Brighton. On 19 August 1989 dozens of members of the public walked to John Street police station, voicing their concern and demanding that the case be re-opened. The three families took part, the bereaved parents side by side with the former accused man, Russell Bishop. The Appeal Fund set up after the murders provided money to print a 'Wanted' poster bearing a coloured illustration of the 'Pinto' sweatshirt, the first occasion in Britain that the demands of public opinion resulted in such a poster being privately published. Its text was written by me. Following these strong expressions of public concern, Mr Roger Birch, Chief Constable of the Sussex Constabulary, promised to take a closer look at the new evidence.

On 12 October 1989, tired of waiting for a reply from the Sussex police, I wrote to the then Prime Minister, The Rt Hon Margaret Thatcher MP, and included some of the case documents and a photograph of the two dead girls taken by Baynes in the Wild Park. A reply was received within days from Lord Ferrers, a Home Office official, stating that he had been instructed to look into the fresh evidence I presented.

On 19 December 1989 Lord Ferrers wrote again, stating that the police had made further enquiries into the deaths and had arranged further meetings with the parents. The significant part of the letter was his statement that the papers had been passed to the Director of Public Prosecutions for his decision on any further proceedings. The suggestion that another individual, acting alone or in concert with a second person, possibly Bishop, might have been responsible for the girls' deaths, appeared to have made an impression. Quite obviously this new evidence was being taken very seriously indeed.

The Assistant Chief Constable (CID) of the Sussex police, Mr R. P. Lind, wrote to me on 2 February 1990 and stated that owing to the strongly circumstantial nature of the new evidence there were insufficient grounds to warrant an arrest. Regional television news, TVS, broadcast that the new investigation had been concluded and that evidence put forward had not been 'quite strong enough'.

Two days later another terrible crime was committed in Brighton.

A seven-year-old girl roller-skating near her home on the Whitehawk Estate, Brighton, was abducted. She was snatched from the street and bundled into the car of a man previously seen working nearby on a motor car. An hour and a half later she was found wandering naked, bleeding and crying through gorse bushes on Devil's Dyke, a West Sussex beauty spot. She fell sobbing into the arms of David and Susan Clifton, a couple out walking, who immediately contacted the Sussex police. The child said that she had been strangled and asked the couple if they were kidnappers too.

Within five hours of the attack being reported, twenty police officers were making their first visit to Bishop's new home at Preston Barracks. He was one of a small number

of suspected sex offenders routinely drawn into the
enquiry team's net. Other suspects were visited at
Eastbourne, Seaford and Gosport. Outside Bishop's home
was a red Cortina with a 'For Sale' sign in the rear window.

Jennie Johnson, not for the first time, shouted at the
officers, 'He was found innocent! All the time you come to
him!' With Johnson hitting out at the police, Bishop was
dragged, protesting his innocence, to a police vehicle and
conveyed to John Street police station where he was later
charged with kidnapping, sexual assault and attempted
murder.

Bishop was at first spoken to by Detective Inspector
Malcolm Bacon and Detective Sergeant Andy Young. At
first he remained calm. Later, in court, he described his
movements during the afternoon of the abduction. He
claimed that at around 3.45 p.m. he had been at his
brother's house in Haybourne Road, Whitehawk, fixing a
television satellite dish, that later he had driven to his
parents' home in Coldean Lane, where he cleaned his car.

Bishop was wary of the police, not least because one of
the arresting officers, D S Young, had investigated the fire-
bombing incident at his house in 1989 after his acquittal
of the Babes in the Wood murders. It was natural in all the
circumstances that Bishop and those defending him for
the Devil's Dyke offences should think it possible that the
police harboured resentment against him. Such allegations were made and, not unnaturally, denied by the
police.

It was Ronald Thwaites QC, Bishop's counsel, who first
made reference to the Babes in the Wood case when he
questioned a witness. The revelation that Bishop had
been tried and acquitted of double murder in 1987 was
reported by the *Evening Argus* to have 'brought a stunned
silence to the packed number in court . . .'

Another echo of the past came when Dr Iain West, the Home Office pathologist, gave evidence. He described the victim of the Devil's Dyke attack as 'lucky to be alive'. She had been throttled into unconsciousness with a sleeper hold* and had probably been left for dead. He thought she was fortunate not to suffer permanent brain damage. Earlier in the proceedings, Dr Martin Knott, the police surgeon, had shown the jury photographs of the girl's injuries. There were bruises round her neck consistent with finger and thumb marks.

Police officers giving evidence were questioned about allegations of prejudice towards Bishop. Asked if he had told Bishop, 'You got away with the last case, but you won't get away with this one,' Detective Inspector Bacon made firm denials. The suggestion that they had had Bishop under regular observation using mobile patrols near his home was also denied.

Detective Chief Inspector Tim O'Connor, the officer heading the Devil's Dyke enquiry, told the court that he was aware of the views in various quarters that Bishop had been wrongly acquitted in 1987. He stressed that he had gone to great lengths, from the time of the first briefing, to emphasise to his men that the two cases should be kept completely separate. He said that he had not even read the files on the earlier case and denied that any exhibit from it had been brought into the present matter. He was unable to explain how a reference to Bishop's blood

---

* Properly known as the carotid sleeper. This hold can only be applied from behind the victim, using the arm bent at the elbow. The upper and lower arm compress both the common carotid arteries but in the crook of the elbow the airway remains unobstructed. The hold causes a temporary lack of oxygen to the brain, resulting in the incapacitation of the victim.

sample from the Babes in the Wood case had turned up
in the files of the Devil's Dyke enquiry. It turned out that
one of the prosecution's forensic experts admitted he
had been given a file containing information relating to
the Babes in the Wood investigation. The file, which
should have been destroyed, contained the results of
blood tests carried out on Bishop. Ronald Thwaites QC
was thus able to make a telling point about the lack of
separation between the two cases. There were other mistakes, too, including a remark made to Bishop that the
police were looking for a red Ford Cortina when all that
was known at the time was that a red car might be impli-
cated. In fact the initial search was for a red Sierra.

Other slip-ups during the early stages of the Devil's
Dyke enquiry bore distant echoes of the 1987 trial in that
they cast doubt on the integrity of some of the forensic
evidence. A pair of green overalls taken from Bishop's
home was put into an evidence bag that was neither
sealed nor labelled by the time it was received at
Brighton police station. A number of references were
made to inadequate procedure regarding the sealing and
logging of exhibits, Ronald Thwaites sarcastically describing the exhibits store at John Street police station as
'a lucky dip'.

On Wednesday, 14 November 1990, The Devil's Dyke
Kidnap Trial, as it was called by the *Evening Argus*,
opened at Lewes Crown Court. Russell Bishop was
described as an unemployed labourer and roofer. He was
charged with kidnapping a seven-year-old girl, commit-
ting indecent assault and attempting to murder her. He
sullenly pleaded 'Not Guilty' to every offence.

Ann Curnow QC, prosecuting counsel, told the court
the evidence showed conclusively that Bishop was the

man who had seized the girl close to her home on 4 February 1990 and locked her into the boot of his red Ford Cortina. The young victim gave her evidence from behind a screen in the court, out of sight of her alleged attacker. Mr Justice Nolan questioned her in a kindly fashion about her age and her favourite school lessons and offered to remove his wig, as he thought the strange headgear might upset her. 'No, that's okay,' she assured him. He decided that she was fit to give evidence and to tell the truth, ruling that she need not take the oath.

In a clear voice, she answered questions put to her by counsel and described the events that Sunday afternoon. She had been out in the street on the Whitehawk Estate, returning from a visit to the sweet shop. She had been dressed in a blue jumper, ski pants and a red and pink anorak and was wearing roller boots. As she skated home she noticed a man working on a red car.

'I was crossing the road,' she said, 'and he jumped out and caught me.' He grabbed her from behind, pushed her into the boot of his car, then drove off.

Because light penetrated the confined space of the boot through a hole by one of the rear lights, the girl was able to locate a hammer which she used to hit the underside of the boot lid in an attempt to attract attention. The man, who was playing the car radio, shouted at her to stop making a noise. She had the presence of mind to take off her roller boots, reasoning that when the boot lid was opened she would have a better chance of escape.

The journey from the point of abduction to the spot where the car stopped at Devil's Dyke took about 25 minutes. It was a fast ride and when the car cornered, the girl was thrown from one side of the boot to the other. When the vehicle stopped at Devil's Dyke the driver dragged her out and, with a hand held over her mouth, pushed her on to the back seat. At this point, as she told the court in her direct way, 'He strangled me.' She lost consciousness. The attacker then sexually abused her and left her for dead.

When she came to, she was lying naked among some gorse bushes. She scratched her body breaking clear of the bushes: 'I was dizzy and kept falling over,' she said. She struggled along a muddy path until she met Susan and David Clifton, who were enjoying the scenery while they drank coffee from a Thermos flask. They saw an 'apparition', a naked, distressed and bleeding child who told them, 'I've been kidnapped.' They covered the shivering girl with a cardigan and jacket and reported her discovery to the police at 5 p.m.

A massive police search was mounted involving nearly 500 officers. The girl told police that the man who had assaulted her had a beard, brown hair, that he was thin and 'middle size'. He was youngish, wore black trousers and something blue. They combed the area where the attack had taken place and found some of the girl's clothing, together with her roller boots, hidden in the roots of a fallen tree. A pair of tracksuit trousers, thought to have been discarded by the attacker, were found by a taxi driver in Mill Road.

A couple who had been walking their dog at Devil's Dyke had noticed a parked red car with steamed-up windows. They assumed it was occupied by a courting couple. There was a notice in the rear window bearing the words 'For Sale £750 ONO'. The last character of the registration number was the letter W. Bishop's car, of course, was red and also bore a 'For Sale' notice in the back window. It later transpired that his red Ford Cortina was a stolen vehicle. Bishop knew this and, like a complete idiot, he still tried to sell it publicly.

The police pointed out that when requested to attend an identification parade where the victim would seek to identify her assailant, Bishop slicked down his hair with copious quantities of water to make it look darker. They ordered Bishop to dry his hair before standing in the line-up. Ralph Haeems was there to protect his client's interests. After the identification parade was completed at the Claremont Centre in Lewes Road, Haeems left despondent in the knowledge that the victim had positively identified Russell Bishop as her attacker. Bishop had been requested to provide intimate and non-intimate body samples (blood and hair). At first he refused, but then agreed. 'I am embarrassed,' he said.

It was inevitable that car paint would enter the Devil's Dyke investigation. It transpired that red particles found on the victim's roller boots, and which subsequently provided vital evidence indicating that the girl had been in Bishop's car, had been removed from the boots before being seen on them by a forensic expert.

Ronald Thwaites used this to suggest that pressure on the police to find incriminating evidence against Bishop was so great that they had been tempted to tamper with evidence, an allegation that was strongly denied. Dr Michael Dabbs, a Home Office forensic scientist, dismissed the suggestion on the grounds that the particles in question were too small for anyone to have gone to the trouble of deliberately planting them. '. . . I would have expected them to put enough in to make sure that the poor misguided scientist was able to pick them up,' he said. Nevertheless, it seemed that the Sussex police had not profited a great deal from the criticism they had received during the Babes in the Wood investigation over the need for scrupulous procedures to maintain the integrity of evidence material.

Counsel claimed that Bishop had been hounded by the police since his acquittal in 1987. 'Were they capable', he asked, 'of dealing fairly with this man? Even if they had wanted to, were they capable?' He told the jury that Bishop could not have committed the attack at Devil's Dyke because he was elsewhere at the time – in other words, that he had an alibi.

At 3.20 p.m. Bishop had been observed in his red Ford Cortina at traffic lights in Coldean Lane. The car in front of him was driven by Christopher Gorring, who confirmed the time, and said that Bishop, whom he recognised, had turned into Middleton Rise when the lights changed. The victim had left her home at about 3.30 p.m. and was seen a few moments later in Haybourne Road. A red car was seen being driven in nearby Wisdon Road at approximately the same time.

Bishop claimed he left his brother's house in Haybourne Road at about 4 p.m. when he was seen in his car by a friend. This friend couldn't be traced by the police. Bishop was seen driving along Coldean Lane and at 5.05 p.m. he was seen outside his parents' house at Coldean. His father, Roy Bishop, refused to make a statement to the police because his experience was that 'They made all sorts of different stories up'. Therefore he could not confirm or deny his son's movements that afternoon.

Defence counsel claimed that the other sightings meant that Bishop could not have been the driver of the red car seen in Whitehawk just before the abduction. Even he could not be in two places at the same time, remarked Ronald Thwaites, adding that Bishop simply did not have the time or the opportunity to kidnap the girl, drive her to Devil's Dyke, assault her, scatter incriminating evidence and be back at his parents' home just over 45 minutes later.

It was forensic rather than circumstantial evidence that was once again the focus of the case. The black tracksuit trousers found in Mill Road carried traces of saliva and semen, both of which were subjected to DNA profiling. The implication was that the wearer of the tracksuit trousers had been sufficiently in contact with the victim for her to have left saliva on them. Bishop denied that the trousers were his and no evidence was adduced to prove that they were. The odds against the saliva having originated from anyone other than the victim were put at 1 in 5.7 million and the chances of the semen not being Bishop's put at 1 in 80 million. The traces were identified as being the girl's and Bishop's.

Fibres found on the tracksuit trousers matched the blue acrylic material of the girl's jumper, supporting the contention that the wearers of the two garments had been in contact. It was initially stated in court that the jumper, bought by the girl's mother as a special offer from Marks and Spencer three days before the attack, was one of only 71 similar garments manufactured, a figure significantly modified when a buyer for the store said that 36,000 of the acrylic jumpers had gone on sale in 225 stores.

Forensic experts had spent two days meticulously examining Bishop's Ford Cortina. They found scratches on the inside of the boot lid which, it was argued, had been made by the victim hammering on the metal to attract attention. They also found a crumpled piece of adhesive tape to which was stuck a single blue fibre measuring three to four millimetres in length, which they said was microscopically indistinguishable from the material of the victim's blue jumper, although they could not say for certain that it had originated from that garment. Their cautious conclusion was that the evidence supported the idea that the piece of tape and the jumper had been in contact. Asked by defence counsel if he might have expected to find more than one fibre, David Northcott said, 'I might have expected to find more. I might not have found any at all.' The reader might be forgiven for thinking this was all a repeat of the Babes in the Wood case.

Dr Dabbs testified that the evidence was consistent with the victim having been in the boot of Bishop's car. Furthermore, tyre impressions found in the ground near the scene of the assault at Devil's Dyke matched the tyres. on the red Ford Cortina, which had three manufactured by Tigar and one by Uniroyal. Despite the most thorough search of the car, no fingerprints belonging to the attack victim were found in the boot or elsewhere, nor were there any of Bishop's fingerprint impressions, as might normally be expected to be the case.

Bishop went into the witness box at Lewes Crown Court on 4 December 1990 and testified for five hours. When cross-examined by Ann Curnow, Bishop again denied all the charges laid against him. Reminded that his semen had been found on the victim's vest and on the discarded tracksuit trousers, he said quite simply that it had been planted. He explained that police had had access to a condom he had recently used at home. Jennie Johnson confirmed that they had had sex on the Saturday night and that the used condoms had been put in a bin in the bedroom. They were still there when police searched the house the following evening. Asked by counsel if the suggestion was that the police had retained one or more condoms and scattered the contents on the garments, Bishop replied, 'Yes, miss.'

Confronted by the evidence that tyre impressions at the scene of the attack matched the tyres of his car,

Bishop answered, 'All I can say is that if they are my tyre marks then I suggest that Detective Inspector Bacon or another officer drove the vehicle up there.'

Defence claims that Bishop had been framed by the police were dismissed by Ann Curnow. She said such allegations were a smoke screen intended to deflect the jury while the facts amounted to a one-way ride to Bishop's guilt. The video of the victim's identification of her assailant had had a considerable impact on the jury when it was shown to them during the trial. One of them told me that none of the jury could believe that this little innocent girl could have lied to the police and acted in accordance with a possible desire to have Bishop 'fitted up'.

Bishop broke down in tears when his counsel questioned him about the Babes in the Wood trial three years previously. He referred to the hate campaign that had been directed against him and Ronald Thwaites asked if he could explain why the police had said they were not looking for anyone else in connection with the double murder.

'Because they believed that I got away with it,' he replied. Thwaites told the jury that his client had become a target for the police within hours of the Devil's Dyke attack, that they had followed his scent remorselessly.

'The police and scientists', he said, 'have strained every fibre and sinew of their being to bring home Russell Bishop's head to you, which some regarded as the missing trophy they failed to get when they were last here.' Mr Thwaites denied attacking the integrity of the police, but said they were there to do a job and if they did it badly they must stand up to criticism.

In his closing speech, Ronald Thwaites asked if the girl attacked at Devil's Dyke had seen one of the posters, in circulation during the hate campaign, bearing Russell Bishop's photograph and calling him a child killer. The implication was that she might have been predisposed to pick out Bishop on the identity parade. He was particularly critical about the handling of the evidence and suggested that anyone with a motive for incriminating Bishop could have gained access to the exhibits, with all the opportunities which that opened up to fabricate evidence against him.

Mr Justice Nolan, in his summing-up to the jury, warned them not to be influenced by the fact that Russell Bishop had been acquitted in the Babes in the Wood murder trial. He gave a careful, considered review of the evidence, a difficult task in view of some of the allegations which had been aired in court. He praised the courage of the victim, but told the jury to bear in mind her age and the shocking ordeal she had been put through. Although she had picked out Bishop at an identity parade, there were dangers in placing undue reliance on her identification. It would be dangerous to convict on her evidence alone, he said. He pointed out that Bishop did not have to prove his alibi – it was up to the prosecution to prove it false. He repeated several times that if they were in doubt as to the defendant's guilt, they must acquit him.

'You must be satisfied beyond all reasonable doubt,' he reminded them. 'Nothing else will do. Anything less than that and the defendant is entitled to be acquitted.' After listening to the evidence for 21 days, the jury of six men and six women retired to consider their verdict.

The jury was out for four hours and twenty minutes. They returned to a packed court. Over 200 people were in the public gallery, including members of the Fellows and Hadaway families. When the verdict of 'Guilty' was announced on the charge of attempted murder, the court erupted into wild cheering and applause. Guilty verdicts were also delivered on the charges of kidnapping and sexual assault. Surrounded in the dock by four prison officers, Russell Bishop, who had proclaimed his innocence throughout, put his head in his hands and sobbed.

Mr Justice Nolan said he could pass only one sentence to match the wickedness of the attempted murder, and that was life. He also imposed two concurrent sentences of ten years each for kidnapping and sexual assault. He told Bishop, 'You are a very dangerous man – perhaps more dangerous than you yourself realise.' The judge praised the police and particularly Detective Inspector Malcolm Bacon, who had been subjected to a great deal of criticism. To the officers involved he said, 'I offer you the commendation of the Bench and the gratitude, I am sure, of the public for solving this crime.'

After the trial, it emerged that a man driving a red car had twice followed an eight-year-old girl in Hollingdean, Brighton, a few days before the Devil's Dyke attack. The young girl concerned had run home and scribbled down the details of the car; it was a red Ford Cortina, registration number TJN 6 something 3 something. It was only after news of the Devil's Dyke attack broke that the significance of the incident was realised. Bishop's car, of course, was a red Ford Cortina, registration number TJN 673 W. Mr Justice Nolan had refused to allow this information to be introduced at the trial on the grounds that it might prejudice his defence.

The prejudice existed, of course, and it was freely aired in the press. The local newspaper, the *Evening Argus*, was restrained in its reporting on the link between the Devil's

Dyke offence and Bishop's acquittal of murder three years earlier, but the national tabloid newspapers had no such inhibitions. In their editions of 14 December 1990, the *Daily Mirror* headline was 'JUSTICE FOR OUR BABES' and the *Sun* carried a picture of Nicola Fellows and Karen Hadaway's grave above the headline, 'I KNOW HE KILLED KAREN'. Both papers referred to the Babes in the Wood case in their lead paragraphs; thus the two cases were inextricably combined in the public mind.

As Bishop was driven away from court in a high-security van to begin his life sentence in solitary confinement, scuffles broke out when photographs were taken of his family. The *Evening Argus* went to press with an edition proclaiming: 'GUILTY: THE SEX BRUTE OF THE DYKE.' One of the parents of the Babes in the Wood murder victims was reported as saying: 'He got what he deserved.'

There had been great mental pressure on Bishop during the final days of the earlier Home Office enquiry. In an unguarded moment he said that he knew he could not be tried again for the Wild Park killings, but that in the back of his mind there were nagging doubts which he could not explain. Two days after the enquiry result was televised on TVS Regional News, a man driving a red Ford Cortina was noted by several children, following them. Two days later Bishop dragged a small girl into his Ford Cortina and tried to kill her.

Perhaps the combination of anxiety and sexual desire brought about a kind of re-play of actions he knew had taken place before, reckoning without the intelligence, strength and resilience of a seven-year-old girl. The pattern was there, of remembered example. Example said clothes should be taken off and thrown away. Was Bishop intelligent enough to have worked out this defensive action for himself? If he understood the reasons for removing clothes, would he not have remembered that tests on clothes that were found could point a finger? Surely the sensible thing would have been to destroy the clothes, especially if the child were dead and there would be no immediate search made, with himself as an obvious target. In that sense, the careless scattering of clothes seems like an echo of dimly remembered precept rather than the act of a calculating murderer who had killed before and got away with it.

Bishop is now in prison, suffering the solitary privations of Rule 43 which protects sex offenders; watched night and day in an ever-illuminated cell, escorted to his meals, to exercise and to the toilet, probably for the remainder of his life, by prison officers who, like the rest of us, want no truck with a child molester. He will live a living death.

It would be convenient to think the Babes in the Wood case could now be allowed to die. This is not possible, except for those who find it convenient to believe in guilt by association. In reality, and in accordance with English Criminal Justice, Bishop's conviction for the Devil's Dyke offences does nothing to alter the facts which governed the botched investigation into the murders of Karen Hadaway and Nicola Fellows.

Despite their satisfaction at the outcome of Bishop's second trial, even the Sussex police entertain doubts about the verdict of the tabloid newspapers. The Babes in the Wood case was still on the files, referred to as 'an unsolved and undetected' murder case. Detective Inspector Malcolm Bacon, who arrested Bishop in 1989, was reported in the *Daily Telegraph* on the day following the end of the Devil's Dyke trial as declaring, 'Police have always said that if someone comes forward with fresh evidence on the Wild Park case, we will look at that evidence.'

Index